Introduction to Medical

...ional
Therapists

WITHDRAWN

Introduction to Medical Law

Peter Marquand
BSc MRCP Solicitor

OXFORD AUCKLAND BOSTON JOHANNESBURG MELBOURNE NEW DELHI

Butterworth-Heinemann
Linacre House, Jordan Hill, Oxford OX2 8DP
225 Wildwood Avenue, Woburn, MA 01801-2041
A division of Reed Educational and Professional Publishing Ltd

A member of the Reed Elsevier plc group

First published 2000

British Library Cataloguing in Publication Data
Marquand, Peter
  Introduction to medical law
  1. Medical laws and legislation — Great Britain
  I. Title
  344.4′1′041
Library of Congress Cataloguing in Publication Data
A catalogue record for this book is available from the Library of Congress

ISBN 0 7506 4239 4

This book is intended as a general reference guide for those in training or in
active practice in the medical profession and professions allied to it. If there
are specific questions regarding any particular issue or problem advice should
be sought from a qualified legal practitioner. Although every effort has been
made to ensure the accuracy of the text, the author and publisher cannot
accept responsibility for any errors or omissions or for the consequences
which might occur as a result.

Printed and bound in Great Britain by Biddles Ltd, Guildford and King's Lynn

FOR EVERY TITLE THAT WE PUBLISH, BUTTERWORTH-HEINEMANN
WILL PAY FOR BTCV TO PLANT AND CARE FOR A TREE.

Contents

Preface

The actions of doctors and other health care professionals are coming under increasing scrutiny and the numbers of complaints and legal claims have increased. My aim has been to produce an accessible text about the law as it relates to medicine in some commonly encountered areas of clinical practice—although it cannot be a substitute for legal advice.

I am very grateful to my friends and colleagues Frances Clift, Lindsay Gee and David Mason at Capsticks and to my friends James Mander FRCS and Helen Reid MRCP FRCR for reading the text and providing helpful suggestions and comments. I should also like to thank Chris Brophy from Capsticks for his assistance and advice during the preparation of the book. Finally, I could not have completed this task without the help and support of my wife, Pauline, and my daughters, Charlotte and Lucy.

The law is stated as at 16 August 1999.

P. Marquand

Introduction

This book is intended to be an introduction and brief guide to the law of England and Wales, illustrating the way in which the law can affect medical practice. It is aimed particularly at those who are closely involved in clinical care. The purpose of the book is to inform practitioners about the legal framework within which they work and treat patients. This is not a fully inclusive guide to the law and certain legal aspects that are not directly concerned with the practice of medicine, such as employment issues, are not included. The book is not meant to be an academic text but tries to demonstrate the practical use of the law by including frequent examples of real and theoretical cases and situations to which, it is hoped, practitioners can relate.

Why is it important to be aware of the law and procedure?

Nearly every day the newspapers report on a medical negligence case that has been settled in the High Court. Frequently, these are obstetric cases when a child has suffered injury during birth. The damages in such cases are often in the region of £1–2 million and can be around £3 million. However, these cases represent the tip of the iceberg. Figures available from the Department of Health reveal that in the period 1991 to 1992 the cost to the National Health Service (NHS) of litigation was £60 million and in the period 1995 to 1996 was approximately £250 million. It is estimated that this will increase by 25 per cent per annum. The total financial liability for the NHS (if all the claims had to be paid today) would be in the region of £2.8 billion.

The Government has encouraged people to complain and the public are now less willing to accept unexpected outcomes without question. The 12.8 per cent rise in the number of complaints to the Health Service Commissioner (Ombudsman) in the period 1993 to 1994 and a 25 per cent increase in complaints to the General Medical Council (GMC) in 1997 compared to 1996[1] are evidence of this trend.

The extent of potential clinical negligence in the UK is unknown. However, the potential number of medical negligence claims in the USA has been demonstrated in a study from Harvard published in the *New England Journal of Medicine*[2]. This showed that in 30,000 randomly selected patients, 3.7 per cent had an adverse outcome whilst in hospital and, of those events, 27.6 per cent were probably due to negligence. This represents an adverse event for approximately 1 in 100 hospital in-patients.

Although the most high profile impact of the law on medicine is in the context of medical negligence (now termed clinical negligence), there are other important areas. Examples of these are the coroner's court, the criminal law, medicinal products, the regulation of the practice of medicine by the GMC and confidentiality. Doctors may have received little or no training with respect to the law in these areas and may not know the legal boundaries of their practice. This creates the risk of an inadvertent breach of the law, and knowledge of the legal framework will help to reduce that risk.

The basis of the law in England and Wales

The law and legal process in England and Wales have evolved over hundreds of years. The Sovereign's power to make the law and judge his/her subjects has been passed down to two separate bodies, Parliament and the Judiciary, respectively. In general terms, Parliament is supreme and the highest law maker.

The law in England and Wales is broken into two basic parts, statute law and common law. The law set out in Acts of Parliament (Statutes) is supreme and overrides any conflict with common law. Statutes often give power to others to make 'delegated legislation', for example, statutory regulations controlling the use of ionizing radiation in X-ray departments. Large portions of the rules and regulations of the GMC consist of this type of law.

The concept of 'the common law' is a set of principles which are applied equally across the country, i.e. common to the land. The roots are hundreds of years old but still set out the law in those areas not covered by Acts of Parliament. An Act of Parliament may specifically replace parts of the common law but if there is no specific provision then, where there is conflict with the common law, the law in the Act prevails.

The system of courts in England and Wales is hierarchical. Decisions made by the higher courts must be followed by the lower courts. This is the system of precedent. For example, any decision made by the highest court, the House of Lords, must be followed by all other courts. The important decisions of the courts are reported and published—for example, in the *All England Law Reports* and on the Internet. These publications record the judgement of the court and are referred to in other cases as they show the legal reasons for a decision.

Civil and criminal law

There is often confusion over the distinction between criminal and civil law. These have different functions, which are outlined below.

The civil law allows individuals redress against each other when legal rights have been or are likely to be affected. The successful outcome to civil litigation is an order requiring or preventing an action (the injunction) or an award of money (damages). In a clinical negligence claim the patient will seek monetary compensation for any loss that they have suffered. The legal consequences of any finding by the court are purely financial. There may, of course, be other consequences such as adverse publicity and damage to the practitioner's reputation. In broader terms, the threat of civil litigation may help to maintain and improve standards.

Civil proceedings are dealt with in the County Court or the High Court, depending on various factors including the value of the claim and the area of law involved. Appeals from these 'courts of first instance' are to the Court of Appeal and then, if necessary, to the House of Lords.

In contrast, the criminal law may be seen as rules set by the State to govern society which must be followed. They are intended as deterrents and the consequences of breaking them are far-reaching and result in punishment. Criminal trials take place in the Magistrates' or Crown Courts depending on the type of offence. Appeals are to the criminal division of the High Court, the Court of Appeal and the House of Lords. Health care staff are rarely charged with criminal offences. However, due to the nature of their practice, they could become involved in cases of murder, manslaughter and assault.

An individual may decide to take a particular course of action which runs the risk of infringing somebody else's rights. If this breaches the civil law there will be no consequences unless the person who has suffered a loss takes action and the successful outcome would be an award of money. However, there are events which can amount to both a civil claim and a crime: for example, assault. In this case, the injured person may recover money and the state may punish the perpetrator.

References

1 *GMC Annual Review* (1998) The General Medical Council
2 Brennan, T.A., Leape, L.L. and Laird, N.M. *et al.* (1991) Incidence of adverse advents and negligence in hospitalized patients—Results of the Harvard Medical Practice Study 1. *New England Journal of Medicine*, **324**, 370–376

2

Who is liable?

When a patient decides to sue they must know the identity of the person or organization to be held responsible. Since 1 January 1990, doctors, nurses and other health care staff in the NHS have been covered by the NHS indemnity, which means their employer is responsible for any clinical negligence claims. For other claims and for those incidents involving private patients, the practitioner concerned is personally responsible.

The NHS indemnity

The NHS indemnity[1,2] covers health care professionals for clinical negligence claims which occur whilst they are working for the NHS. The indemnity defines 'health care professional' as including:

'Doctors, dentists, nurses, midwives, health visitors, hospital pharmacy practitioners, registered ophthalmic or registered dispensing opticians working in a hospital setting, members of professions supplementary to medicine and dentistry, ambulance personnel, laboratory staff and relevant technicians'.

It excludes GP practices, general dental practices, pharmacies and opticians' practices.

The term 'clinical negligence' is defined as:

'A breach of duty of care by members of the health care professions employed by NHS bodies or by others consequent on decisions or judgements made by members of those professions acting in their professional capacity in the course of employment, and which are admitted as negligent by the employer or are determined as such through the legal process'.

The cover is retrospective and therefore applies to claims that arise out of incidents that occurred before the date indemnity came into force. The indemnity is wide, as can be seen, but it does not cover all the possible activities of a doctor employed by the NHS or anything that does not amount to 'clinical negligence'—for example, category 2 work such as insurance company reports (see page 7).

In terms of the legal process against an NHS defendant, it does not matter precisely who is to blame if there has been negligence, for example, if the failure was by the senior house officer (SHO) or supervising registrar, or by the nursing staff or a combination of personnel. If the patient can establish negligence somewhere, they will succeed and there is no need to apportion the responsibility. Of course, it would be important to establish where any failing occurred so that lessons could be learnt from the incident to reduce the risk of repetition.

However, the various staff involved in an incident are vital to the process, even if they are not personally being sued. The Trust or Health Authority is carrying the financial responsibility for its actions and cannot defend a claim without evidence, which must come from the individuals concerned.

The NHS body responsible will carry out the necessary investigations and it will have its own solicitors to deal with the claim. The various staff involved do not require their own legal representation in these circumstances but are always free to contact their own defence organizations or trade union for advice if necessary.

Any claims that are made where the date of the alleged negligence is after an NHS Trust was created falls to the Trust. If the negligence occurred before the Trust's formation, then the Health Authority is the correct defendant. For example, Dr X has been a consultant since 1980 at a hospital that is part of an NHS Trust which was formed on 1 April 1994. Negligent treatment is alleged whilst a patient was being seen at the hospital on 5 May 1989. The correct defendant is therefore the Health Authority.

The National Health Service Litigation Authority

In 1996 the Government set up the National Health Service Litigation Authority (NHSLA) to co-ordinate defence litigation and to promote risk management.

There are two schemes run by the NHSLA. First, the existing liabilities scheme (ELS) operates where the alleged negligence took place before 1 April 1995 and secondly, the clinical negligence scheme for Trusts (CNST) is used for claims after that date. Trusts and Health Authorities have to report claims to the NHSLA to take advantage of the scheme, which will meet the damages and legal costs beyond certain thresholds.

Activities not covered by the indemnity

Individuals will be personally liable for those activities which do not fall within the NHS indemnity.

Examples of this include the following:

1. General practitioners and general dental practitioners are not covered. However, a general practitioner who works as a clinical assistant in an NHS hospital will be covered for any clinical negligence arising from that post.
2. Private practice is not covered, whether the patient is in an NHS hospital or a private hospital. However, if the patient is in an NHS hospital and the staff are retained by the NHS to look after the private patients, they will be covered by the indemnity. For example, the consultant will not be covered but the nurses and junior staff will be if it is part of their medical job to look after the private patients.
3. 'Good Samaritan' acts, for example stopping to help at the scene of an accident, are not covered.
4. Criminal proceedings are not covered even if they occur in the course of treating NHS patients.
5. Disciplinary proceedings or proceedings taken by a professional body are not covered—for example, a doctor will not receive any assistance if he is called to appear before the GMC.

For example, an anaesthetist carries out a private list in an NHS hospital. He or she would be the correct defendant for an alleged act of anaesthetic negligence.

Given the limitations of the indemnity, it is advisable to have in place additional defence cover with one of the medical defence organizations. Furthermore, such cover is a requirement of the GMC set out in the booklet *Good Medical Practice*[3] and the Government has said that it will be made a legal obligation for doctors. Individuals working for private hospitals or clinics should also examine their indemnity position to make sure that they have adequate cover in the event of a claim.

Summary

A clinical negligence claim occurring whilst working for the NHS will mean that the NHS body will take the responsibility. In all other cases the individual will be responsible and should have suitable indemnity arrangements.

References

1 Department of Health (1989) *Claims of Medical Negligence Against NHS Hospital and Community Doctors and Dentists.* HC (89) 34
2 NHS Executive (1996) *NHS Indemnity—Arrangements for Handling Clinical Negligence Claims Against NHS Staff.* HSG (96) 48
3 General Medical Council (1998) *Good Medical Practice*

Clinical negligence

When a patient brings a medical negligence claim it will be in the civil court. In order to succeed the following three factors must be established:

1. The practitioner owed the patient a duty of care.
2. There was a breach of the duty of care.
3. The breach of the duty of care caused a loss (causation).

Duty of care

A prerequisite to a successful legal claim is that the person or institution being sued owed a duty of care to the injured person. The duty must be one recognized by the law as giving rise to a liability. The doctor–patient relationship creates such a legal duty to take care and this is not usually a controversial point in clinical negligence claims. However, it could be relevant if the doctor alleges that the claimant was not his patient. For example, if the relative of a patient brings a claim the doctor may not, in certain circumstances, owe them a duty of care[1]. There is also no duty towards an injured person passed in the street, although once a doctor provides assistance in such a case a duty of care arises.

Breach of duty

Anyone who asks a professional person to do a job expects it to be done properly, whether by a plumber, electrician or doctor. The legal standard that professionals must meet is the standard of the ordinary skilled person exercising and professing to have that special skill. In clinical negligence cases a judge assesses whether or not that standard has been reached and for this he requires independent evidence from somebody who also possesses the particular skill. For example, it would be difficult for a judge to establish whether a hysterectomy had been properly performed without the opinion of a gynaecologist.

In medical cases the standard is met if it is accepted as proper by a responsible body of medical opinion. This is the formulation known as the 'Bolam test', named after the case in which it was applied[2].

In practice what does this test mean? In any medical negligence case the opinion of experts (usually consultants) who practice in the same speciality as the doctor who is accused of negligence will be required. For example, assessing the clinical standard of a neurosurgeon should be done by other neurosurgeons rather than by orthopaedic surgeons. These experts represent the 'responsible body of medical opinion'.

In most jobs/professions there is more than one way of performing a task and perhaps this is especially true in medicine. Doctors may offer different diagnoses for a particular set of symptoms or have differing opinions on how and when a particular treatment should be given. This is reflected in the law so that a judge cannot find negligence just because he prefers one doctor's opinion over another[3]. There is no negligence if the acts or decisions not to act are accepted clinical practice, which may even represent a minority view, even if there is an honestly held contrary view[4].

Although the court takes into account the expert's evidence it is the court that makes a finding of negligence and not the expert doctors. It is a mistake to think that all that is required to defend a claim is the support of a consultant. The existence of a common practice in a profession does not automatically mean that negligence cannot be found. For example, it might make economic sense to send out ships with insufficient places in lifeboats for all the passengers and crew, but the fact that all ship owners followed this practice would not stop it being wrong. The House of Lords has commented on 'Bolam' in the case of 'Bolitho'[5]. Cases subsequent to 'Bolam' used different adjectives to describe the 'body of medical opinion', such as 'responsible', 'reasonable' and 'respectable'. In 'Bolitho' the House of Lords said that these words all amounted to the same thing and meant that the court had to be satisfied that the 'body of medical opinion' withstood logical analysis. Lord Browne-Wilkinson stated: '...the court has to be satisfied that the exponents of the body of opinion relied on can demonstrate that such opinion has a logical basis. In particular, in cases involving, as they often do, the weighing of risks against benefits, the judge before accepting a body of opinion as being responsible, reasonable or respectable, will need to be satisfied that, in forming their views, the experts have directed their minds to the question of comparative risks and benefits and have reached a defensible conclusion on the matter.' For example, a judge is unlikely to accept an expert's opinion that it was acceptable to withhold thrombolytic therapy from a patient presenting with an acute myocardial infarction (who had no contraindications) on the basis that the consultant did not believe in its efficacy. The judge does not have to accept, without question, the expert's opinion, which must be reasonable and justifiable.

An example of this approach comes from the cases that arose out of the problems with a cervical screening programme in Kent[6]. Three women had cervical smears between 1989 and 1992 which were all reported as negative by cytoscreeners. Two expert cytopathologists gave evidence for the patients and three for the defendant. All the experts agreed that, except for one slide, given the increase in understanding of cytopathology, the smears would have been reported as abnormal at the date of the trial. However, the defendant's experts were of the view that, at the time the smears were taken, a negative report was not negligent. Nevertheless, all the experts agreed that when a cytoscreener had any doubt about whether a slide was normal or abnormal it should be passed on and classified as abnormal. The judge applied the Bolam test to the case as explained in 'Bolitho' and found against the defendant despite there being supportive expert evidence. The judge rejected the views of the defendant's experts that the cytoscreeners had made understandable errors in interpretation of difficult slides and he did not think it was logical to classify a slide as normal when there was any doubt about the report because of the potential consequences of a mistake.

How high is the standard?

It would be unreasonable to expect medical practitioners of all levels to reach the standard of a professor in a teaching hospital. The standard set by the law is that of the competent post holder, so that a senior house officer (SHO), for example, has to reach the standard of a reasonably competent SHO[7]. Whether this standard has been reached will depend on the expert evidence.

There are two qualifications to the standard. First, a junior doctor should realize the limits of his knowledge and skill. Any failure to refer a case for a more specialized or senior opinion may be found to be below an acceptable standard[7]. Of course, whether or not the patient successfully sues will depend on other facts and subsequent events, such as whether the actions of the senior doctor (to whom the junior doctor referred the patient) reached an acceptable standard and/or whether the doctors' employer was negligent for not employing suitably experienced staff.

For example, a premature baby treated on a special care baby unit developed retrolental fibroplasia and had severe visual loss. The premature baby had required oxygen and in order to monitor the oxygen level a catheter had been inserted. Unfortunately, inadvertently, a vein was catheterized rather than the artery. The procedure had been carried out by a junior doctor and a check X-ray had been performed which was thought to be satisfactory. The doctor had asked the senior registrar to check the placement of the catheter, which he did, but no abnormality was detected. The court found that the junior doctor was not negligent in his mistake as he had appropriately referred to a senior person. However, the senior registrar was found to have been negligent for failing to detect the incorrect placement on the X-ray[7].

The second qualification to the standard is that no allowance is made for beginners and it is not a defence to a claim of negligence to argue that the doctor's actions were appropriate for somebody who had just started their post[8]. Any shortcomings should be dealt with by adequate supervision. This seems harsh on beginners who often have to learn 'on the job' but from the patient's point of view it makes sense that they should be able to expect to be cared for by a competent or adequately supervised practitioner whenever they attend for treatment.

Causation

The patient must show that any breach of duty that has been established has caused a loss, otherwise the claim will fail. This will not pose a problem when the case is clear-cut, such as an operation on the wrong leg, for example. However, the patient has to establish that the loss that has been suffered was caused by the negligence (i.e. breach of duty) and not the underlying disease. For example, a casualty officer did not see a patient who attended with vomiting due to arsenic poisoning and from which the patient later died. A breach of duty was established because the doctor failed to see the man but the claim failed because, even if the patient had been seen and admitted, the antidote could not have been administered quickly enough to be effective[9]. In other words, the negligence could not be said to have caused the death, which was due to the poison.

However, the breach of duty does not have to be the only cause of the loss but it must be a material cause. If there is more than one possible cause, the burden remains on the patient to prove that it was the breach of duty that led to the loss. For example, in the case of retrolental fibroplasia referred to above, there were other possible natural causes for the condition and the House of Lords stated that it was up to the patient to prove that it was the misplaced catheter and high levels of oxygen that had caused the condition in order to recover damages.

A similar argument to the one above has been used in cases where doctors have omitted to act in circumstances where they should have done. If the outcome would have been unaltered had the doctor acted, then the failure to act will not have caused a loss to the patient. In these circumstances, the doctor's proposed actions must also satisfy the Bolam test.

This was the situation in the Bolitho case[5] referred to above. A two year old boy was admitted to the paediatric ward with croup. At 12.40 p.m. he had an episode which caused the nursing staff concern about his respiratory state and the case was discussed with the senior registrar who said she would attend. Approximately 1 hour and 20 minutes later a second episode occurred and the senior registrar was called and the SHO was asked to attend. In between these episodes of respiratory difficulty the boy was pink and playing. About half an hour later the boy had a respiratory arrest which, despite resuscitation, resulted in severe brain damage. Unfortunately, the boy died some time later. It was established that the senior registrar's failure to attend or to arrange for somebody else to attend was a breach of duty. However, if she had attended she stated that she would not have intubated the boy, which the experts agreed was the required course of action that would have avoided the ultimate outcome. The defendant's experts supported this approach on the basis that there was only a small risk of total respiratory failure compared with the risk of the invasive procedure of intubation. This analysis passed the test set out above and the defendant was not held liable.

A patient has to prove the cause of their loss on a balance of probabilities, i.e. it is more likely than not (greater than 50 per cent in statistical terms). This may pose difficulties for the patient if the loss is one that could have occurred anyway as a result of the disease. For example, a boy who fell out of a tree and suffered a slipped epiphysis later developed avascular necrosis. The defendant Health Authority admitted that there had been negligence because of a delay in diagnosing the epiphyseal injury, but the patient did not succeed in his case. The reason for this was that there was a 75 per cent chance that avascular necrosis would have occurred even if the injury had been diagnosed immediately. He was unable to prove that it was more likely than not that the delay in diagnosis caused the avascular necrosis[10].

Res ipsa loquitur

Res ipsa loquitur means 'the thing speaks for itself' and is applied to circumstances where it may be inferred that there is no explanation for an occurrence other than a negligent one. For example, an amputation of the incorrect leg could, on the face of it, have no reasonable explanation and negligence can be inferred from the fact of its occurrence. Res ipsa loquitur is often raised in clinical negligence cases, in particular in cases where an outcome is difficult to explain. A defendant can overcome the presumption of negligence if it can be shown that proper care was exercised or if there is a non-negligent explanation for what occurred. The explanation must be a plausible one and not a theoretically or remotely possible one[11].

For example, a woman's ureter was damaged during an hysterectomy. From the expert evidence there were three possible explanations, two of which could only have occurred by negligence and one, namely unintended kinking of the ureter caused by a nearby suture, that could occur with or without negligence. The judge accepted that this was the likely mechanism of the damage but found negligence on the basis that, in general, a negligent cause of kinking was more likely, on the balance of probability, than a non-negligent cause. In effect, the defendant could not win because the judge had determined as a fact (on the balance of probabilities) that all three possible causes of damage to the ureter could only occur by negligence, which amounted to res ipsa loquitur. The Court of Appeal overturned this decision on the basis that the judge's reasoning was flawed. The patient had to prove that, in her case, the damage was caused by negligence, which the court said she had failed to do[12].

Loss

It is usually the loss which starts a claim. A patient who has an unexpected outcome may investigate the possibility of compensation. There may be cases where a patient's perception of their loss is greater than any actual loss. An example of this is a delay in the diagnosis of cancer. Assuming that the outcome is the same, then compensation would be for the pain and suffering (and perhaps psychiatric consequences) between the date at which the diagnosis should have been made and the time that it actually was made. If there is no loss at all then the claim will fail.

The patient must have suffered a loss to bring a claim and it is the loss that receives compensation. The aim of the law in this context is to put the patient back in the position that they would have been in had negligence not occurred. Compensation for any physical injury will include an award for the pain and suffering and the loss of amenity (known as general damages). The court also awards a sum for any past and future financial losses that have been caused by the negligence. This will include lost earnings, and the costs of care, aids and equipment, for example. In fact, any loss that can be shown to have resulted from the negligence, such as the development of a psychiatric illness, may be claimed as long as it is not too remote. In cases where the damages are very high, most of the money will have been awarded for future loss—for example, the total package of future care for a child with cerebral palsy may be in the region of £1.9 million or more. However, the award for the catastrophic brain injury itself may only be a relatively small part, at around £110,000–150,000.

Summary

In order to defend a clinical negligence claim, when a duty of care is owed to a patient, the treatment given must have reached an acceptable standard as judged against accepted practice that is able to withstand logical analysis. If the treatment does not meet the required standard any such failing must have caused a loss to the patient for the claim to be successful.

References

1 Powell v Boladz [1998] Lloyd's Rep Med 116
2 Bolam v Friern Hospital Management Committee [1957] 1 WLR 582
3 Maynard v West Midlands Regional Health Authority [1985] 1 All ER 635
4 Defreitas v O'Brien [1995] 6 Med L R 108
5 Bolitho v City and Hackney HA [1997] 4 All ER 771. Text in quotations copyright Reed Elsevier UK Ltd, reproduced by permission of the Butterworths Division of Reed Elsevier (UK) Ltd
6 Penney, Palmer and Cannon v East Kent Health Authority [1999] Lloyd's Rep Med 123
7 Wilsher v Essex Health Authority [1986] 3 All ER 801
8 Nettleship v Weston [1971] 3 All ER 591
9 Barnett v Chelsea and Kensington Hospital Management Committee [1968] 1 All ER 1068
10 Hotson v East Berkshire Health Authority [1987] 2 All ER 909
11 Ratcliffe v Plymouth and Torbay Health Authority [1998] Lloyd's Rep Med 162
12 Hooper v Young [1998] Lloyd's Rep Med 61

4

Crime

This chapter is not intended to cover crimes in general but to look at those crimes with which a doctor or other health care professional may become involved during the course of their practice. Assault, murder and manslaughter are crimes that a doctor might come into contact with because the nature of their practice inevitably involves those elements that could constitute these crimes in other circumstances. As indicated in the introduction to this book, the procedure for criminal law is different to that in a civil claim. Criminal cases are investigated by the police with the evidence being passed to the Crown Prosecution Service (CPS) who decide if the case is to proceed. Any subsequent trial would proceed through the Magistrates' Court and/or Crown Court, depending on the nature of the offence.

The elements of a crime

Before dealing in detail with some specific crimes it is necessary to look at the basic elements of a crime which are applicable to all offences. Each crime comprises two parts: the actus reus and the mens rea.

Actus reus

The actus reus is the act or omission that constitutes a crime. For example, in murder the act of killing or in assault (see below) the physical contact with the individual.

Mens rea

Mens rea is the mental element of a crime. An assault is not an assault unless the attacker uses physical force intentionally or recklessly. For example, people in a crowded train constantly knock into one another. The acts constitute the actus reus of assault but there is no mens rea.

The mental elements that exist for offences are:

- Intentionally: An act done on purpose.

- Recklessly: An act which carries an unjustifiable risk of causing an adverse outcome. The perpetrator might be aware of the risk or it may be a situation where he/she ought to have been aware of it.
- Negligently: Failing to take reasonable care whilst carrying out an act.

The law specifies which mental element is required (it may be that any one of the three will be sufficient) for an offence to have been committed. At the trial, the judge will direct the jury on the legal definition of the necessary mens rea and the jury will have to decide, in coming to a verdict, if the defendant had the necessary mental element.

The burden of proving the constituent parts of a crime falls to the prosecution. The jury have to be satisfied 'beyond all reasonable doubt' about the facts, which amounts, effectively, to certainty.

Assault and other offences against the person

In normal usage an assault is taken to mean any physical contact with another person. However, the legal definition of an assault is any act which intentionally or recklessly (the alternatives, which are the mens rea) causes the victim to apprehend immediate and unlawful personal violence. No touching of the victim is required for an offence to have been committed. If there is any contact, however slight, then the crime is one of battery. The distinction between the two is important as they are different crimes, but in the text below the word 'assault' will be used throughout.

In general terms, the more serious the injury that is inflicted by an assault, be it physical or mental, the more serious the crime. The spectrum extends from an assault occasioning actual bodily harm to the offences of wounding or grievous bodily harm. When the skin has been breached the injury suffered fulfils the definition of a wound, while 'grievous' is defined as meaning 'really serious'.

In day to day practice health care professionals constantly carry out the acts that would constitute an assault, for example abdominal palpation, or more serious crimes such as wounding when performing an operation. What makes the difference is the presence of a patient's consent to the procedure (see Chapters 5 and 6) and that the ultimate aim of the procedure is to do good and not harm the patient.

Homicide

Patients may die during or as a result of treatment. The death can therefore be incidental, accidental or amount to the crimes of manslaughter or murder (collectively termed homicide).

Murder

The crime of murder occurs when a person's death is caused by someone who intends to kill or cause him grievous bodily harm. The distinction between murder and manslaughter is the intention to kill or cause really serious injury. The jury in a trial may find that the defendant intended to kill or cause grievous bodily harm when that was his purpose or when the death (or really serious injury) was a virtually certain consequence of the action and the defendant knew that to be the case[1].

A person may be found guilty of murder even if the victim was dying from another cause. For example, it would still be murder if a patient with terminal cancer was killed deliberately by any means. However, the situation is different when a patient dies because of the effect of a drug given to relieve pain, as it is part of the doctor's role to alleviate suffering. If the primary purpose of administration is to relieve pain and suffering then administration will be lawful even if death is hastened (sometimes referred to as 'double effect'). If this were not the case, then a lot of palliative treatment would be unlawful. However, a jury will be directed to examine the facts closely and if a drug does not have analgesic properties, or is administered at a dose which is known to be fatal, it is likely that intention to kill will be found despite a claim that relief of suffering was the purpose of administration.

For example, a doctor was found guilty of attempted murder having given an injection of potassium to a patient who was dying in constant pain which did not respond to conventional treatment. The patient was known to be in the process of dying and was perhaps very close to death. She was suffering from very severe pain to the extent that she had asked the doctors to give her an injection to end her life. The doctor was held in high regard and had told the patient that she would not be in pain. After injections of conventional analgesics and sedatives the patient was injected with potassium chloride and died shortly thereafter. The doctor was charged with attempted murder as the prosecution accepted that they could not prove that the potassium was the cause of death in the circumstances of the case. The jury returned a guilty verdict. In his summing up the judge told the jury to disregard the doctor's possible motive for giving the injection and that it made no difference that the patient wanted to die or that at some point a fatal injection had been requested. Motive is not the same as intent[2].

There is an ethical debate about euthanasia but as the law stands at present, as can be seen from the above, it is not lawful to kill another person and there is no exception for the medical profession, even when a patient wants to die and agrees to being killed: consent is not a defence to a murder charge.

A patient may, for any reason, decide that they will take their own life and that is not a criminal offence, although it used to be. However, it is a crime to help or assist in any way with another person's suicide. For example, it would be a criminal offence for anyone to deliberately prescribe sufficient drugs for a patient with terminal cancer to end their own life. It is, therefore, not lawful to achieve euthanasia by an indirect route.

Unlike other offences, the sentence of life imprisonment for a person found guilty of murder is mandatory and the judge has no discretion.

Manslaughter

When a person kills another in circumstances that would amount to murder, the law reduces the crime to manslaughter if the defendant was either (1) provoked or (2) suffering from diminished responsibility. A person may also be guilty of manslaughter when, whilst carrying out a dangerous and criminal act, a person is killed. None of the above should apply to health care workers in day to day practice.

A person may also be guilty of manslaughter when somebody dies because of gross negligence. There must be a duty of care owed to the victim and that duty must have been breached, causing the victim's death, just as for civil negligence claims. The jury has to decide if the conduct reached the required standard of care. If it did not, then they must decide whether, 'having regard to the risk of death involved, the conduct of the defendant was so bad in all the circumstances as to amount, in their judgement, to a criminal act or omission'[3].

For example, an anaesthetist was found guilty of manslaughter when he failed to identify that the patient had become detached from the ventilator. Unobserved, the endotracheal tube had become detached and, after about four and a half minutes, the blood pressure monitor automatically alarmed. The anaesthetist carried out various procedures including the administration of atropine for bradycardia, but was found not to have checked the endotracheal connection prior to the patient suffering a cardiac arrest. The prosecution's expert witnesses described the standard of care as 'abysmal' and stated that the conduct amounted to 'a gross dereliction of care'[3].

Summary

The chances of a health care professional becoming involved with the criminal law are very low in everyday practice. However, the treatment of a patient could fairly easily amount to a crime: for example, treatment in the absence of a patient's consent. The treating clinician's motive will not help evade criminal responsibility.

It is very unusual for clinicians to be charged with manslaughter. Successful prosecutions are extremely rare. The jury must be satisfied that the conduct amounted to something much worse than the negligence required to make a successful civil negligence claim. Furthermore, the prosecution have to prove the case 'beyond all reasonable doubt', which is a much higher standard than the 'more likely than not' basis required in civil negligence claims.

References

1 Smith, J. (1996) *Smith and Hogan Criminal Law*, 8th Edn, p. 58. Butterworths
2 R v Cox [1992] 12 BMLR 38
3 R v Adomako [1994] 3 All ER 81. Text in quotations copyright Butterworth and Co. (Publishers) Ltd, reproduced by permission of the Butterworths Division of Reed Elsevier (UK) Ltd

5

Consent to treatment—negligence and assault

Consent to treatment is a very important area. Defects in consent potentially lead to two legal claims, assault and negligence. As a general rule,
any touching of another person without their consent, however slight,
will be an assault. Therefore, from even the most minor procedure
such as taking a patient's blood pressure, to the most major surgical
operation, the patient's consent must be obtained beforehand.

In order for a consent to exist the following are necessary:

1. The patient must have the necessary capacity to consent to treatment.
2. The patient must have been given sufficient information.
3. There must have been no duress or undue influence on the patient
   in coming to his/her decision.

Capacity

The following chapter deals with capacity to consent to or to refuse
treatment in detail.

Sufficient information

This information includes the reason for the treatment, the nature of
the procedure, likely outcomes and possible treatment alternatives, as
well as information about adverse effects. Failing to give a patient
sufficient information may have two legal consequences: first, assault
and secondly, negligence.

Assault

A failure of information which results in the patient not understanding the general nature of the treatment/procedure means that there is
no consent at all and carrying out the treatment would therefore be
an assault. For example, a dentist carried out extreme treatments on
eight patients when none of them had been given information on which
to base a suitably informed consent. In fact, the patients' teeth were

healthy and the treatment was unnecessary. The judge found that the dentist had withheld information deliberately and in bad faith. The patients had perfectly healthy teeth filled and crowned and had undergone root canal treatment. These treatments amounted to assault as there was no consent[1].

Negligence

If enough information has been given to enable the patient to understand the general nature of the procedure but not the associated risks and options, then this failure may amount to negligence. For example, a consultant anaesthetist was referred a patient who had developed intractable pain around the site of a scar following a hernia operation. He found that the pain was temporarily relieved by injections of local anaesthetic and steroids. He decided to use an intrathecal pain block injection to control the patient's pain. This was used on two occasions and an area of numbness was produced as well as weakness of the patient's leg. Unfortunately, the pain from the scar remained unaffected by the treatment.

The patient claimed that she had not been given an explanation of the procedure or its implications, which amounted to an assault, and that the inadequate explanation was also a breach in the duty of care owed to her by the anaesthetist (i.e. negligence). The judge held that the patient had been informed in broad terms of the nature of the procedure and that there was no assault[2].

In the majority of cases where a problem is alleged to have occurred in the consenting process, assault would not be an appropriate claim as the allegations are usually concerning the failure to warn of a risk. Such failures are categorized as a failure in the consenting process and amount to negligence. However, if the patient is to succeed in recovering damages they also have to prove causation as in any other negligence claim. In other words, the patient has to prove that if they had been given the piece of information they would not have undergone the procedure. Obviously, if they would have undergone it anyway, there is no loss to be claimed. This is a matter of fact to be proved at trial. The patient may well say that they would not have had the treatment but a judge may not accept that evidence. For example, if the procedure was required to save the patient's life, it is unlikely that they would refuse treatment because of a relatively rare complication.

In the example given above of the woman with intractable pain, her case was that if she had been warned of the risk of weakness and numbness in her legs she would have refused the procedure. The judge held that she was a woman who was desperate for pain relief and that the reasons she gave in evidence for potentially refusing the

operation would have been the same even if she had been warned of
the possible complications: these reasons did not include any concern
about numbness or weakness (and, in any event, the judge found that
she had been warned). Consequently, her claim failed[2].

How much information is sufficient?

As indicated above, the patient only has to have been told of the
nature of the procedure in broad terms for the practitioner to avoid
a claim of assault. To avoid negligence in the consent process the
information has to pass two tests. First, the information given must
be supported as being reasonable (i.e. capable of withstanding logical analysis) by a responsible body of medical opinion and secondly,
warnings of any significant risks that would affect the judgement of a
reasonable patient must have been given[3]. Guidance on what a 'responsible body of medical opinion' would support will come from literature,
current textbooks and the practices of the Royal Colleges and the General Medical Council[4]. However, when giving warnings, the doctor can
take into account all the circumstances, which include the ability of the
patient to understand and their physical and mental state. Withholding information solely on the basis that the patient would not consent
to the procedure if they were told the information is very unlikely to
be defensible[4]. The weight of current medical opinion is against the
'doctor knows best' approach.

There can be no hard and fast rule about what amounts to a significant
risk. It has been suggested that it means a risk that was so obvious that
no prudent medical professional could fail to warn of the risk, save in
an emergency or for some other sound clinical reason[3]. For example,
the risk of losing the sight in an eye would be an extremely significant
event to a patient who had sight solely in that eye and, although the
risk of this complication may be remote, it is likely to be expected
that a warning should be given of any such risk. In cases that have
been decided, the judges have referred to risks of about 10 per cent as
amounting to significant risks[3,5]. However, as said above, this is not
a hard and fast rule. Much lower percentages may be significant for
certain individuals depending on the circumstances. Furthermore, if a
body of medical opinion such as a Royal College states that a particular
risk or level of risk should be included in any warning, then a court
is likely to follow that decision as representing a responsible body of
medical opinion. For example, many surgeons warn patients about risks
of 1 per cent or more.

As can be seen from the above, in general, there is no duty of full
disclosure of information to the patient and there is no doctrine of

informed consent in English law as there is in the United States of America. However, if a patient asks for information then those questions must be answered honestly and fully[3]. Furthermore, it is generally accepted that full disclosure should be given to patients taking part in research, including the information that they are part of a clinical trial.

A seventy-one year old female patient had a laminectomy and facetectomy because of pressure on a nerve root causing pain in her right arm and shoulder. She was warned that the operation might damage the nerve root but not that it could damage the spinal cord with a risk of paralysis or that it was an operation of choice rather than necessity. After the operation the patient was paralyzed. The expert medical evidence was that a body of medical opinion would not have warned of the risk of paralysis. This then overcame the first hurdle, to avoid a finding of negligence. The risk of such paralysis was also found to be less than 1 per cent and, in the circumstances, it was not a substantial risk that the patient should have warned about and, therefore, the court did not find there to have been any negligence[3].

A woman was expecting her sixth child. At term plus 14 days she begged the consultant to perform a caesarean section. The consultant advised that she proceed to a normal vaginal delivery. Tragically, the child died in utero before delivery. The court looked at the risk of such an occurrence, which, on the evidence, was very remote at 0.1–0.2 per cent and found that it was not significant and that the doctor did not have to warn of that risk. However, the outcome of the trial might have been different if this was the woman's first pregnancy following a history of several miscarriages or if she had undergone fertility treatment. In those situations, it seems more likely that the risk of fetal death would be considered significant even if the statistical risk remained small[5].

Does the occurrence of a recognized complication avoid a finding of negligence?

Doctors may believe that when a recognized complication of a procedure occurs, they automatically cannot be found to have been negligent. However, this will depend on two factors: first, the consent process would have to withstand expert opinion and analysis by the court and secondly, the complication would have to have occurred without negligence. A finding of negligence cannot be avoided if a procedure is carried out negligently even if the result is a recognized complication. For example, injury of the ureter is a well-recognized complication of hysterectomy. But, even if the patient has been warned, she will recover damages if she can prove that the hysterectomy was performed negligently, resulting in a damaged ureter.

Who can obtain the consent?

In terms of the legality of the consent, it does not have to have been taken by the person who is to perform the operation. An SHO can obtain the consent of a patient to an operation to be performed by a consultant, for example. However, the risk of a patient receiving inadequate information will increase with the inexperience of the person obtaining the consent. Risk management procedures may require consent to be obtained by a person who can perform the procedure. This is also an issue of professional conduct for doctors, as the GMC guidance on consent[4] states:

> 'If you are the doctor providing treatment or undertaking an investigation, it is your responsibility to discuss it with the patient and obtain consent, as you will have a comprehensive understanding of the procedure or treatment, how it is carried out, and the risks attached to it. Where this is not practicable, you may delegate these tasks provided you ensure that the person to whom you delegate:
>
> - is suitably trained and qualified;
> - has sufficient knowledge of the proposed investigation or treatment, and understands the risks involved;
> - and acts in accordance with guidance in this booklet.
>
> You will remain responsible for ensuring that, before you start any treatment, the patient has been given sufficient time and information to make an informed decision, and has given consent to the procedure or investigation.'

Recording the consent

For a consent to be legally valid there is no requirement for it to be in writing (except for some specific cases such as consents under the Human Fertilization and Embryology Act 1990) and an oral agreement would be sufficient. In fact, consent is often taken to exist because of the circumstances, such as offering an arm when a blood sample is requested. This is often called 'implied consent'. Practitioners should be sure, however, that the patient does understand what the proposed treatment or investigation entails.

The reason it is important to have a patient's consent in writing is as a record, so that at a later date it can be shown that the patient went through a consenting process. A patient may have forgotten that they were consented or were given any warnings and the doctor may not be able to specifically remember what was said. Consent forms fulfil the function of recording the consent but they usually do not have a section to record the details of any discussion and identification of risks. It is advisable to record the discussion, including the options discussed and warnings given in detail, and this is particularly the case if the risks for the particular patient deviate from the norm. A tick next to the word 'consent' in the patient's notes is just about better than nothing but will not help if it is alleged that a specific warning should have been given.

Not all procedures or treatments have the consent recorded on a separate form. It is always advisable to write in the notes that consent was obtained and the details as described above, but the use of a separate consent form is a matter of risk management. Minor procedures which do not have potentially serious consequences, such as phlebotomy, represent a low risk in terms of any issue arising out of obtaining the patient's consent and therefore a form would be less useful (and, given the frequency of the procedure, a hindrance). However, an operation under general anaesthetic carries a greater risk of complications and therefore a form is justified. Experience and professional opinion will govern which procedures require a form and certainly forms are being used now for a wider range of procedures than previously.

It is important to appreciate that the consent form has no 'magical' properties. Just getting a signature on the form will *not* mean that consent has been obtained if the necessary conditions for consent to exist have not been met.

Summary

A patient's consent to treatment is a vital component in the management of their condition. Patients need to have sufficient information to enable them to make a choice. The law expects patients to have been warned to the standard expected of a responsible body of medical opinion, which must include warnings of significant risks.

References

1 Appleton and other v Garrett [1996] PIQR P1
2 Chatterton v Gerson [1981] QB 432
3 Sidaway v Board of Governors of the Bethlem Royal Hospital and the Maudsley Hospital and others [1985] 1 All ER 643
4 General Medical Council (1998) *Seeking Patients' Consent: The Ethical Considerations*
5 Pearce v United Bristol Healthcare NHS Trust [1999] PIQR P53

6

Capacity to consent to or to refuse treatment

In order for there to be a valid consent, a person must have the necessary capacity to give that consent. Adults (i.e. those aged eighteen and over) and minors aged sixteen and above are deemed to have capacity to consent unless the contrary is shown. However, minors are not considered in law to be able to make a binding refusal of treatment.

Determining capacity

The first aspect to the consenting process is to determine whether the patient has capacity. In the vast majority of cases this will not pose a problem. It may be clear that the patient does have capacity because of the observations made during the consultation. In other cases it will be clear that they do not—in extreme cases because they are unconscious or obviously confused.

The courts have formulated a test to assess mental capacity, which will have to be specifically applied in cases where there is any doubt. This test may be set out as follows:

'a person lacks capacity if some impairment or disturbance of mental functioning (which may be permanent or temporary) renders the person unable to make a decision whether to consent to or refuse treatment. Such inability to make a decision will occur when:

1. The patient is unable to comprehend and retain the information which is material to the decision, especially with regard to the likely consequences of having or not having the treatment in question; and/or
2. The patient is unable to use the information and weigh it in the balance as part of the process of arriving at the decision. If a compulsive disorder or phobia from which the patient suffers stifles belief in the information presented to him/her then the decision may not be a true one.

Confusion, shock, fatigue, pain and drugs may reduce or completely erode capacity but those concerned must be satisfied that such factors are operating to such a degree that the ability to decide is absent. Another such influence may be panic induced by fear. Again, careful scrutiny of the evidence is necessary because fear of an operation may be a rational reason for refusal to undergo it. However, fear may also paralyze the will and thus destroy the capacity to make a decision[1].'

A patient may fail the capacity test because they cannot understand the consequences of not having the treatment. For example, an adult with learning disabilities may not comprehend that urgent treatment of a fracture/dislocation of his/her ankle is required to restore the blood supply. However, such a patient may be able to comprehend less complex procedures, for example having a blood sample taken. It is possible for a patient to have capacity for some treatments and not for others.

Treatment in the absence of capacity

How then is any adult patient treated lawfully if they cannot consent? Nobody is able to consent on behalf of an adult, not even the court, but the court can declare proposed treatment to be lawful (see below). It is often thought that the next of kin can consent but this is *not* correct. The legal solution is based on the doctrine of necessity.

In the absence of capacity it is lawful to give treatment that is in the patient's best interests. Treatment that is in a patient's best interests has been defined as treatment which is carried out in order either to save life or to ensure improvement or prevent deterioration in physical or mental health: in other words, it is necessary[2]. In addition, the treatment must be supported by a responsible body of medical opinion (i.e. the Bolam test; see Chapter 3). In fact, where an adult patient is unable to consent and is in need of treatment, as described above, the law is that such treatment must be given.

Therefore, if a hypoglycaemic diabetic patient arrives unconscious in casualty, there is no need to worry about obtaining consent before injecting glucose (in the absence of an advance refusal; see below). He or she clearly cannot consent and the treatment is necessary to save life—which would fulfil the best interests definition above.

However, this does not provide carte blanche to allow any treatment. Only that which is immediately necessary should be given to a patient who is likely to regain capacity. If any part of the treatment can wait, then it should do so until the patient can be consented appropriately. For those patients who do not have capacity and are unlikely to regain it, careful consideration should be given to whether any proposed treatment is necessary and in their best interests. Certain treatments require an application to the court, in any event, when the patient does not have capacity and these include sterilization and transplantation[3].

Minors

The position for patients who are aged below eighteen years (i.e. minors) is different to that of adults. For the purposes of consenting to treatment (as opposed to refusing it), minors aged sixteen and seventeen are treated as adults.

In the case of minors below sixteen, there are a variety of individuals who can give consent to treatment, as described below.

The holder of parental responsibility

The mother is always a holder of parental responsibility. The father will also have parental responsibility if he was married to the mother at the time of the child's birth (this is subject to review). Alternatively, the mother may have given the father parental responsibility, but this must have been in the form of a legal document or court order. It is not an informal arrangement. Other people may hold parental responsibility as well; for example, if there is a care order under the Children Act 1989 then Social Services have parental responsibility. It may also have been given by the court to other relatives, again by way of a formal court order. Consent from any one of the holders of parental responsibility will be sufficient.

The child

In certain circumstances the child can give a valid consent to treatment. In order for the consent to be valid the child must have sufficient understanding and intelligence to enable him or her to understand fully what is proposed, i.e. have capacity (known as 'Gillick competence' after the leading case[4]). It is logical that a child who has sufficient understanding and intelligence should also pass the capacity test as set for adults.

Whether a child has capacity will be a matter of fact in each case.

The court

In cases concerning minors (including sixteen and seventeen year olds) the court has the power to consent on behalf of a child and in place of the parents when the child/parents refuse treatment. In doing so, it will exercise that power in accordance with the best interests and welfare of the child. It is unusual to find a minor who is still a ward of court, but if a ward requires treatment then the court's permission must be obtained in any event.

For example, a fourteen and a half year old girl attends gynaecological out-patients without her mother or her stepfather. She is 14 weeks pregnant and is requesting a termination of pregnancy, which could be lawfully performed (see Chapter 13). She does not want her parents to be informed of her condition.

If the girl has sufficient intelligence and understanding of the nature and purpose of a termination and the consequences (social etc.) of the procedure, then it would be lawful to proceed with her consent alone. However, before doing so, the law expects that the clinicians will seek to persuade the under-sixteen year old to inform her parents. This would be easiest on a practical level as well, as it would be difficult if the mother asked for an explanation of the treatment because the child's confidence must be respected by the health care staff.

If the circumstances were different and, say, the child could not consent, then a consent from the mother would be effective. The step-father's consent would not be useful unless the mother had formally shared parental responsibility. The father could consent if he was married to the mother at the time of the child's birth. If the mother or other holder of parental responsibility refused to consent and it was thought that the termination was in the child's best interests, then an application to the court should be made for the court to give consent (or otherwise depending on the court's decision as to the best interests of the child).

Refusal of treatment

Adults

An over-eighteen year old with mental capacity may refuse treatment for any reason, rational or irrational, or for no reason at all[5]. If an adult refuses treatment, then the key is to determine if they have the capacity to consent to or to refuse treatment. If the patient's condition is such that capacity may not be present, then the test set out above should be applied. If there is any doubt as to capacity then, ideally, this assessment should be done by a consultant psychiatrist. However, urgency of treatment may not allow this to be done and, in these circumstances, the assessment should be carried out by the most senior and experienced doctor available.

If the patient has capacity then the law is clear: the refusal must be observed. However, the patient must have been given a complete explanation of the consequences of the decision, including the risks of death and serious injury. A failure to do this would mean that the patient's decision was not based on all the relevant information. The patient's refusal should be documented in full, including what was said and the detail of the doctor's explanation, as well as the fact that the patient had capacity and the reasons for coming to that decision. If possible, this should be witnessed by another doctor or health care professional and signed by the patient. The reason for this is that it would be useful evidence at a later date if there was an inquiry or investigation.

The same considerations apply to a patient taking their own discharge against medical advice. Hospitals often have forms for patients and staff to sign in these circumstances. However, the form is only evidence of a consultation. It has no special properties (as is also true of the consent form, as described in Chapter 5). A patient's wish to go home against advice is the same as a refusal of treatment and should be treated in the same way. Even in the presence of a signed form, a patient who later came to harm could recover damages if he/she had not been warned of a risk which later materialized and the patient proved that if he/she had been told of that risk he/she would not have left the hospital.

If the adult does not have capacity then the law is clear. They should be treated according to their best interests. No consent form is necessary.

Cases where capacity is unclear

There will be cases where the issue of whether or not the patient has capacity is unclear. In these circumstances legal advice should be obtained and an application to the court for a declaration may be necessary. The Court of Appeal has issued guidelines[6] on when to make such applications. The relevant extracts are as follows:

> 'This advice also applies to any cases involving capacity when surgical or invasive treatment may be needed by a patient, whether female or male. References to "she" and "he" should be read accordingly. It also extends, where relevant, to medical practitioners and health practitioners generally as well as to hospital authorities.
>
> The guidelines depend upon basic legal principles which we summarise:
>
> 1. They have no application where the patient is competent to accept or refuse treatment. In principle a patient may remain competent notwithstanding detention under the Mental Health Act.
> 2. If the patient is competent and refuses consent to the treatment, an application to the High Court for a declaration would be pointless. In this situation the advice given to the patient should be recorded. For their own protection hospital authorities should seek unequivocal assurances from the patient (to be recorded in writing) that the refusal represents an informed decision: that is that she understands the nature of and reasons for the proposed treatment, and the risks and likely prognosis involved in the decision to refuse or accept it. If the patient is unwilling to sign a written indication of this refusal, this too should be noted in writing. Such a written indication is merely a record for evidential purposes. It should not be confused with or regarded as a disclaimer.
> 3. If the patient is incapable of giving or refusing consent, either in the long term or temporarily (e.g. due to unconsciousness), the patient must be

cared for according to the [doctor's/NHS Trust's etc.] judgement of the patient's best interests. Where the patient has given an advance directive, before becoming incapable, treatment and care should normally be subject to the advance directive. However, if there is reason to doubt the reliability of the advance directive (for example it may sensibly be thought not to apply to the circumstances which have arisen) then an application for a declaration may be made.

Concern over capacity:

4. The [doctor/NHS Trust etc.] should identify as soon as possible whether there is concern about a patient's competence to consent to or refuse treatment.
5. If the capacity of the patient is seriously in doubt it should be assessed as a matter of priority. In many such cases the patient's general practitioner or other responsible doctor may be sufficiently qualified to make the necessary assessment, but in serious or complex cases involving difficult issues about the future health and well-being or even life of the patient, the issue of capacity should be examined by an independent psychiatrist, ideally one approved under section 12(2) of the Mental Health Act. If following this assessment there remains a serious doubt about the patient's competence, and the seriousness or complexity of the issues in the particular case may require the involvement of the court, the psychiatrist should further consider whether the patient is incapable by reason of mental disorder of managing her property or affairs [see Chapter 14]. If so the patient may be unable to instruct a solicitor and will require a guardian ad litem [person to represent their interests] in any court proceedings. The [doctor/NHS Trust etc.] should seek legal advice as quickly as possible. If a declaration is to be sought, the patient's solicitors should be informed immediately and if practicable they should have a proper opportunity to take instructions and apply for legal aid where necessary. Potential witnesses for the [doctor/NHS Trust etc.] should be made aware of the criteria laid down in Re MB[1] and this case, together with any guidance issued by the Department of Health[7] and the British Medical Association[8].
6. If the patient is unable to instruct solicitors, or is believed to be incapable of doing so, the [doctor/NHS Trust etc.] or its legal advisors must notify the Official Solicitor and invite him to act as guardian ad litem [person to represent their interests]. If the Official Solicitor agrees he will no doubt wish, if possible, to arrange for the patient to be interviewed to ascertain her wishes and to explore the reasons for any refusal of treatment. The Official Solicitor can be contacted through the Urgent Court Business Officer out of office hours on 0171 936 6000.'

The hearing

The patient should be represented at any hearing before a judge as any order made in his/her absence circumstances will not be binding on the patient. A declaration granted in the absence of the patient (known as ex parte) will be of no assistance to the doctor/NHS Trust.

The judge must be provided with all the relevant information, which must be accurate:

'This should include the reasons for the proposed treatment, the risks involved in the proposed treatment, and in not proceeding with it, whether any alternative treatment exists, and the reason, if ascertainable, why the patient is refusing the proposed treatment. The judge will need sufficient information to reach an informed conclusion about the patient's capacity, and, where it arises, the issue of best interest.'

The guidance continues:

'9. The precise terms of any order should be recorded and approved by the judge before its terms are transmitted to the [doctor/NHS Trust]. The patient should be accurately informed of the precise terms.
10. Applicants for emergency orders from the High Court made without first issuing and serving the relevant applications and evidence in support have a duty to comply with the procedural requirements (and pay the court fees) as soon as possible after the emergency hearing.'

Conclusion:

'There may be occasions when, assuming a serious question arises about the competence of the patient, the situation facing the [doctor/NHS Trust] may be so urgent and the consequences so desperate that it is impracticable to attempt to comply with these guidelines. The guidelines should be approached for what they are, that is guidelines. Where delay may itself cause serious damage to the patient's health or put her life at risk then formulaic compliance with these guidelines would be inappropriate.'

Refusal by under-eighteen year olds

Although patients below eighteen may consent to treatment in certain circumstances (as set out above) the law does not recognize their refusal as binding. In theory, the consent of a holder of parental responsibility would be sufficient to protect a doctor legally even if an under-eighteen year old with capacity was refusing treatment. However, the more mature the minor, the more difficult it could be to effect treatment, and before embarking on treatment in these circumstances legal advice should be obtained.

If the holders of parental responsibility refuse treatment of their child but the child has capacity and consents (i.e. Gillick competent or sixteen or over and no evidence of not having capacity), then the treatment can proceed on the basis of the minor's consent alone.

If the minor and holders of parental responsibility refuse or the parents of a non-competent minor refuse treatment which is believed to be in the child's best interests, then an application to the court should be made for the court to consent.

Practicalities

In all cases where capacity to consent is an issue, full records should be kept so that decisions may be justified at a later date. It can seem like a 'no win' situation when decisions have to be made when urgent treatment is needed, as criticism could arise for treating or not treating. What should be recorded is not just the decision, but the reasons and justification for the decision. For example, an opinion that a patient does not have capacity should be supported by the reasons for that assessment. This type of information will help support a decision if it is challenged at a later date as, no doubt, the details will have been forgotten.

For example, a pregnant adult presented to a hospital at term and in labour. She was fully dilated but in arrested labour. Without either a forceps delivery or a caesarean section the baby would die and the mother would be at risk from the danger of the retained fetus. As the woman had previous caesarean sections there was also a risk of scar rupture if the labour was allowed to continue.

The woman, who had a previous psychiatric history, denied that she was pregnant. A consultant psychiatrist's assessment was that, although not suffering from a mental disorder within the meaning of the Mental Health Act, she was not capable of weighing the information about the proposed treatment in the balance to make a choice. The hospital applied to the court for a declaration on the lawfulness of the proposed treatment.

The judge held that the psychiatrist's assessment meant that the woman did not have mental capacity. He also found that ending the labour was in the woman's best interests as without delivering the fetus the mother's physical health would have been put at risk. The judge therefore declared that the treatment was lawful without the woman's consent[9].

An important feature of this case is to realize that the best interests test rests on the *mother* and not the unborn child. In English law the unborn child has *no* legal rights and therefore cannot be taken into account. If a mother who has mental capacity decides, on the basis of the necessary information, that she does not want a caesarean section then that decision would have to be observed. This would be the case even if the fetus was likely to come to harm or die, as it is the mother who determines what happens to her own body.

A further example is as follows. A sixty-eight year old chronic paranoid schizophrenic developed gangrene in his foot, with a grossly infected leg and necrotic ulcer covering the whole of the dorsal aspect of the foot. The surgeon considered that a below-knee amputation was necessary to save the patient's life. The patient refused. As a consequence, a less drastic procedure was performed which resolved the situation temporarily but, ultimately, it was considered that an amputation would be required to save the patient's life. The patient maintained his refusal and requested that the hospital confirm that it would not operate on any future occasion. The hospital refused to agree to the request and legal proceedings were started.

Despite evidence that the patient suffered from grandiose delusions including a belief that he was a doctor of international renown who had never lost a patient, the judge held that, on the evidence, the patient had understood and retained the relevant treatment information and believed it and had arrived at a clear choice. This meant that the patient's refusal must be respected now and in the future[10]. As stated above, an underlying mental condition does not necessarily mean that a patient does not have capacity and an analysis must be made in each case.

Advance directives

It follows from the above example that an adult patient's refusal of treatment may be binding on the doctors even if the event requiring treatment arises at some time in the future. Such advance refusals are commonly referred to as 'advance directives'.

In order to be binding[11] an advance directive must be:

1. Made by someone with the necessary capacity.
2. Applicable to the circumstances that arise.
3. Understood by the patient, who has fully appreciated the significance of their refusal of such treatment.
4. Made without duress.

The example given above of the schizophrenic patient fulfils these criteria: he had capacity and made a decision based on full information about a possible future occurrence. However, consider the situation where a woman before a gynaecological operation makes it clear that she does not want a hysterectomy. The planned procedure occurs without incident but several weeks later she presents unconscious with several weeks of vaginal bleeding which can only be stopped by performing a hysterectomy.

At the time of her refusal, when she had capacity, did she envisage the fact that a hysterectomy would be the only way of saving her life? Information from the family members may help to clarify the situation (but note they cannot consent or refuse treatment on her behalf). It seems likely in these circumstances that the patient would not have considered the circumstances that later arose and, therefore, she should be treated according to her best interests. Clearly, the decision in all such cases will depend on the particular facts.

Advance directives are quite common and the standard NHS consent form contains a section for patients to record procedures that they do not want to happen without their express consent. A more complex situation arises when, a significant time in advance of an event, or in anticipation of an event, a patient has made an advance refusal of treatment. An example might involve Jehovah's Witnesses refusing blood transfusions, even in life-threatening circumstances. If such a refusal fulfils the criteria set out above, then it will be binding and any treatment in contravention of the refusal would be an assault.

In considering whether an apparent advance directive is effective, it is worth considering the following:

1. Is there any question about the patient's mental capacity at the time of the decision?
2. What are the family's views on what the patient would have wanted (but remember to consider confidentiality here)?
3. Is there any evidence that the family/individual(s) put pressure on the patient to make a particular decision?
4. Was the patient aware of the consequences of the decision and the risks/benefits?
5. Do the circumstances that have arisen fit with the circumstances envisaged when the advance directive was made? For example, a refusal of treatment X in any circumstances may not be binding if the patient did not consider at the time of making the advance directive the circumstances that have in fact arisen.

There is no legal requirement for any advance directive to be in writing but, obviously, it is a lot easier to establish whether it fulfils the criteria if it is written. The British Medical Association has published a Code of Practice[12] which includes advice on such drafting. Legal advice should be obtained if there is uncertainty over an advance refusal of treatment.

In the circumstance of elective treatment a clinician may not be prepared to give treatment on the terms requested by the patient. For example, a Jehovah's Witness who needs a hysterectomy may have made it clear, in advance, that she refuses any blood transfusions during the operation. The surgeon must respect that woman's wishes but he/she may feel that they cannot operate on those terms. In these circumstances it would be appropriate to help the patient find another surgeon who would be prepared to operate.

This above example raises another important principle. A doctor cannot be forced to treat a patient. Therefore, a patient cannot say that they want or demand a particular type of treatment, and any such statements are not legally binding. It may, however, be appropriate to take such statements into account when considering what treatment is in a patient's best interests in the event that they cannot be consulted.

There is also no basis in the law of England and Wales for a third party who has been appointed by the patient to make treatment decisions on their behalf. The statements of such people, whatever their legal sounding title, are not binding. However, again that is not to say that their opinions on what the patient would have wanted are not a relevant consideration. Occasionally those people to whom an enduring power of attorney has been given (see Chapter 14) believe they can consent to medical treatment; however, this is *not* correct.

Sometimes documents that contain requests for positive treatment and/or the apparent appointment of another to make decisions are referred to as a 'living will'. The terminology is not universally applied and therefore it is important to look at the text to determine if there are any refusals of treatment, as these may be legally binding.

In general terms, unless the advance directive is clear and unambiguously fits the circumstances, it would be advisable to take further advice on the effect of any refusal or living will. For example, there would be little room for doubt where the doctor and patient had discussed the treatment options beforehand and a decision has been reached. However, a patient unknown to the staff presenting with an advance directive creates a more uncertain position.

Medical intervention against a person's wishes

The law does provide that, in certain very limited circumstances, a person may be admitted to hospital against their will. These circumstances are as outlined below.

1. For the purposes of securing the necessary care and attention for those persons who:
   (a) are suffering from grave chronic disease or, being aged, infirm or physically incapacitated, are living in insanitary conditions; and
   (b) are unable to devote to themselves, and are not receiving from other persons, proper care and attention[13].
2. In order to have someone medically examined by a doctor if there is reason to believe the person is or has been suffering from a notifiable disease[14]. Alternatively, an individual who is thought to be a carrier of a notifiable disease or a group of individuals, if there is reason to believe that one of them is a carrier, may be examined. The medical examination must be in the person's (or people's) own interests or that of his (or their) family or in the public interest. In the case of testing an individual, the examination can only be ordered if the person is not being treated by a doctor or, if he or she is being treated, then the doctor's consent must be obtained. Medical examination

in this context includes bacteriological and radiological tests and 'similar investigations', which are likely to include blood tests[15].

3. A person who is suffering from a notifiable disease may be taken to hospital if proper precautions are not being taken (or cannot be taken) and if there is a serious risk of infection to others[16].

Summary

An adult patient with mental capacity is free to agree to or refuse medical treatment. Patients aged sixteen and seventeen may consent to treatment, as may any child who has the necessary understanding although their refusal is not binding. For under-eighteen year olds there are various ways of obtaining valid consent, including applying to the court. The key to determining whether a consent or refusal to treatment is genuine is whether a patient has mental capacity. In cases of doubt it may be necessary to apply to the court.

References

1 Re MB [1997] 8 Med LR 217
2 In re F (Mental Patient Sterilization) [1989] 2 WLR 1025
3 Practice Note [1996] 2 FLR 111
4 Gillick v West Norfolk and Wisbech Health Authority [1985] 3 All ER 402
5 Sidaway v Board of Governors of the Bethlem Royal Hospital and the Maudsley Hospital and others [1985] 1 All ER 643
6 St George's Healthcare NHS Trust v S [1998] 2 FLR 758. (Also available on the Internet and extracts appear in the Health Service Circular from the NHS Executive (1999) *Consent to Treatment—Summary of Legal Rulings*. HSC 1999/031.)*
7 NHS Executive (1999) *Consent to Treatment—Summary of Legal Rulings*. HSC 1999/031
8 British Medical Association (1999) *Withholding and Withdrawing Life-Prolonging Medical Treatment—Guidance for Decision Making*. BMJ Books. (Also available on the Internet.)
9 Norfolk and Norwich Healthcare (NHS) Trust v W [1997] 34 BMLR 16
10 In re C (Adult: Refusal of Treatment) [1994] 1 WLR 290
11 Re T [1992] 3 Med LR 306
12 British Medical Association (1995) *Advance Statements about Medical Treatment*. BMJ Publishing Group
13 National Assistance Act 1948, section 47
14 Notifiable Diseases: section 10 of the Public Health (Control of Disease) Act 1984 and the Public Health (Infectious Disease) Regulations 1988, SI 1988/1546
15 Public Health (Control of Disease) Act 1984, sections 35 and 36
16 Public Health (Control of Disease) Act 1984, section 36

7

Withholding and discontinuing treatment

In the vast majority of cases withholding and discontinuing treatment will not pose a problem as it can be discussed with the patient. However, in certain types of cases the decision may be extremely difficult, for example, in those patients where death would result if the treatment were to be stopped but they are not actually in the process of dying, or withholding treatment in those who do not have the necessary mental capacity to make treatment decisions.

This is a controversial and difficult area of law unless the patient is irretrievably in the process of dying from their illness. Legal advice should be obtained in any circumstances where it is proposed to withhold or withdraw treatment, the effect of which would be to hasten death. It is important to appreciate that artificial hydration and feeding is considered to be treatment for these purposes. Furthermore, the guidance produced by the Royal College of Paediatrics and Child Health[1] should be consulted, as should the guidance from the British Medical Association (BMA)[2]. There is a very strong presumption in the law that preservation of health and life is in a patient's best interests and this can conflict with individual practitioners' ethics and what they believe to be in the patient's best interests. The circumstances must be very special for the law to sanction steps opposite of those which would preserve life and result in the patient coming to harm and eventually dying. However, there is no obligation in law on medical staff to keep a patient alive at all costs and regardless of the circumstances. Whatever the doctor's motive, any deliberate withholding or withdrawing of a treatment which causes a patient's premature death could amount to murder, and hence the need for caution in this area.

The law recognizes that life-saving treatment may be withheld or withdrawn in those patients unable to make their own decisions in the following circumstances:

1. Where the patient's life will be intolerable.
2. Where the treatment is futile.
3. Where administration of the treatment is not practically possible.

Although broken down into these groups, they are all based on whether the treatment is in the best interests of the patient and the BMA guidance[2] refers to whether the treatment gives a 'net benefit'. Any action should be capable of being supported by a responsible body of medical opinion.

Where the patient's life will be intolerable

The position of the patient may be such that their life is intolerable or would be so if the treatment were to be administered. What must be determined, as best it can, is what the patient would find intolerable—and not what another person might think of as being intolerable. Factors to take into account are the existing disability and any additional suffering or aggravation of the disability to which the treatment would lead[3].

For example, a baby born at 27 weeks of gestation suffered recurrent apnoeic attacks that required ventilation. He had suffered extensive hypoxic brain damage at birth. The medical evidence was that he was likely to be blind and deaf and a spastic quadriplegic, and the prospect of even limited intellectual ability was very unlikely. His life expectancy was greatly reduced. Despite these disabilities the evidence was that he would have been able to feel pain. The decision had to be made as to whether he should be ventilated again if he had a further apnoeic attack.

The court decided that, although there was a strong presumption in favour of preserving life, there were circumstances where withholding life-saving treatment would be appropriate. The medical opinion was against further ventilation except in the event of a chest infection. The court balanced the increased length of life that might be achieved by ventilation, the nature of ventilation and the associated procedures and the effect of those steps on the child and the child's present quality of life. The court decided that, in this case, ventilation could be withheld if the child stopped breathing unless the doctors treating him thought it appropriate to ventilate in the clinical circumstances[3].

Where the treatment is futile

In some cases the treatment would be futile because the patient is already in the process of dying and the treatment would not alter that chain of events and would confer no benefit[4]; for example, a patient with terminal disseminated cancer who develops a chest infection. The question of the time frame is important because it comes down to assessing the balance of what effect the treatment would have against the effect of the treatment itself and whether it is in the patient's best interests. If a practitioner does not feel that any such decision to withhold or withdraw treatment would be supported by a large body of informed and responsible medical opinion then legal advice should be obtained. For example, a sixty-five year old woman with widespread carcinoma develops a chest infection and needs ventilation in order to save her life. The medical evidence is that, if her chest infection is treated with antibiotics and ventilation, it is likely that she will recover even though, probably as a result of the cancer, she will die in a few months. Given the strong presumption in favour of preserving life, in the law it is likely that, in such circumstances, a court would not find it lawful to withhold antibiotics or ventilation. Such treatment could not be said to be futile.

Patients who are brainstem dead but on a ventilator may have the ventilation switched off. The brainstem death should be established in the appropriate manner but there is no need in these circumstances to seek any other advice. The patient is dead and the treatment does not give any benefit and, in effect, the patient has no interest at all in living.

The law also recognizes that patients who are in a permanent vegetative state (PVS) may be allowed to die by withdrawal of treatment including artificial hydration and nutrition. However, in contrast to the above, an application to the court should be made[4,5].

Before any application to the High Court is made the following steps need to have been taken[5]:

1. The diagnosis should have been made and the guidance from the Royal College of Physicians followed[6]. PVS cannot be said to exist in cases of head injury unless the vegetative state has been present for 12 months or 6 months in the case of other aetiologies such as a stroke.
2. Rehabilitation should have been attempted.
3. Reports on the patient's condition should have been prepared over time.
4. The views of the next of kin and relatives should have been obtained.
5. The Official Solicitor should be involved and usually he represents the patient. One of the Official Solicitor's functions is to act on behalf of patients who are unable to make decisions and represent their interests.
6. At least one independent report (i.e. in addition to that of the treating consultant) will need to have been commissioned from a neurologist or other specialist in conditions like PVS. The Official Solicitor will also commission a similar report.

7. Legal advice should have been obtained on the details of the application to ensure the necessary steps have been satisfactorily completed.

The basis for withdrawal of hydration and feeding is that PVS is a state where the patient is alive with a functioning brainstem but without higher cerebral function. The patient is dependent for their existence on being fed artificially but there is no prospect of recovery. In such circumstances the decision has to be made on the basis of the best interests test but in the circumstances of PVS the treatment is useless. The prolonging of life is futile because there is no prospect of recovery and the state of PVS is not one of benefit to the patient. The withdrawal of feeding is not akin to starvation as the feeding has to be provided by artificial means and is similar to the use of ventilation for breathing. The law has not considered those patients who are not in PVS, for example with strokes, and legal advice should be sought in such cases if it is thought that withholding or withdrawing artificial hydration and nutrition would be in the patient's best interests.

The well-known case of Anthony Bland[4] which arose out of the Hillsborough disaster resulted in the first legal decision regarding the withdrawal of artificial feeding from a person in PVS which had lasted for three and a half years following a crush injury that had led to hypoxic brain damage. He had been subject to extensive rehabilitation efforts but to no avail. He did not demonstrate any cortical brain activity on EEG. Although he was able to breath spontaneously he required nasogastric feeding and hydration and was totally dependent on others for his care. There was no hope of any improvement. The court found that artificial feeding and hydration was medical treatment and sanctioned its withdrawal on the grounds summarized above, even though it would lead to his death.

Where the treatment is impractical

It may be that the circumstances are such that giving the life-saving treatment to a patient who is not co-operative who does not have capacity would be impractical. This must be a very rare situation. However, again the basis behind the decision is likely to be what is in the patient's best interests.

For example, a forty-nine year old chronic schizophrenic developed chronic renal failure and needed haemodialysis three times a week. He did not have the mental capacity to consent to or to refuse the treatment but he did refuse it. In those circumstances it would be lawful to administer the haemodialysis in the absence of consent as it is needed to save his life and is, therefore, in his best interests. However, the patient refused the haemodialysis and behaved in such a way that it would only have been possible to give the treatment if he were under general anaesthetic on each occasion that dialysis was required. Some force would have had to have been used on those occasions to administer the anaesthetic. Each of the general anaesthetics carried a significant risk to the patient's health. In those circumstances the court declared that it would be lawful not to administer the haemodialysis because of the practical difficulties[7].

Summary

Except in cases where a ventilated patient is brainstem dead or withdrawal of treatment is proposed in a patient who is irretrievably in the process of dying from their illness, legal advice should be sought before taking any action. In the case of patients in PVS an application to the court will be required. Of course, withdrawal or withholding of treatment does not mean *no* treatment, and care and medication should be given to alleviate any suffering and discomfort.

References

1 Royal College of Paediatrics and Child Health (1997) *Withholding or Withdrawing Life Saving Treatment in Children—A Framework for Practice*
2 British Medical Association (1999) *Withholding and Withdrawing Life-Prolonging Medical Treatment—Guidance for Decision Making*. BMJ Publishing Group. (Also available on the Internet.)
3 Re J (a minor) (Wardship: medical treatment) [1990] 3 All ER 931
4 Airedale NHS Trust v Bland [1993] 1 All ER 861
5 Practice Note [1996] 4 All ER 766
6 The permanent vegetative state. Report by a Working Group convened by the Royal College of Physicians and endorsed by the Conferences of Medical Royal Colleges and their Faculties of the United Kingdom (1996) *Journal of the Royal College of Physicians, London*, **30**, 119–121. See also: Addendum to a review by a Working Group convened by the Royal College of Physicians and endorsed by the Conferences of Medical Royal Colleges (1997) *Journal of the Royal College of Physicians, London*, **31**, 260
7 Re D (Medical Treatment: Mentally Disabled Patient) [1998] 2 FLR 22

8

The Mental Health Act 1983

This chapter deals with the law surrounding the treatment of patients suffering from mental disorders. It covers compulsory admission to hospital for assessment and treatment and emergency powers. This is an area of medical practice that is highly regulated by the law as it concerns the liberty of the subject and allows treatment of the mental disorder without consent in certain circumstances. This chapter is a summary of the main provisions and is not intended to cover all that a practitioner in psychiatry might need to know. In practice, psychiatrists should take legal advice if in doubt as to the legality of their actions when dealing with a patient suffering from mental illness.

The provisions of the Mental Health Act 1983 (MHA) allow for the compulsory admission to hospital and treatment of patients suffering from a mental disorder. The MHA sets out the requirements that have to be met before a patient can be admitted and treated and allows the patient and their 'nearest relative' opportunities to oppose the compulsory admission. It provides a framework which is intended to safeguard the patient from abuse of power. Under the MHA the Secretary of State for Health has published a Code of Practice[1] and this gives guidance to practitioners on how to apply the MHA.

The two most frequently used provisions are section 2 (admission for assessment) and section 3 (admission for treatment). Both sections have similar procedural requirements. There must be an application for admission made by either the patient's nearest relative or an approved social worker. The application must be founded on the written recommendation of two doctors who must include the particulars required by the relevant section of the MHA. There are special forms which must be used for the section 2 and section 3 applications and the accompanying doctors' reports. The two doctors may assess the patient together or separately but the gap between their assessments must not exceed five days[2].

Various people have important functions within the MHA which are common to the different sections. The roles of these various people will now be considered.

The nearest relative

The MHA sets out who the nearest relative is according to a list[3] and it is the function of the social worker to determine who is the nearest relative for the purposes of the MHA application. In any particular case the patient's nearest relative will be the person who appears first on the list. There are various factors to be taken into account; for example, gender is irrelevant and the eldest of any relatives in the same category takes precedence.

There may be occasions when the person who is the nearest relative does not feel able to take on the responsibilities. The MHA allows for delegation to take place[4]. The situation may also arise where the nearest relative objects to a proposed admission which is considered to be in the interests of the patient. The MHA has a provision for replacement of the nearest relative following an application to the County Court[5].

Approved social worker

A social worker has to be specifically approved to carry out the required duties under the MHA. The approved social worker must make an application under the MHA if he is satisfied that an application ought to be made and is of the opinion, having regard to any wishes expressed by relatives, that it is necessary and proper for him to make the application[6].

The social worker must interview the patient before making an application under the MHA and be satisfied that the detention in hospital is, in all the circumstances, the most appropriate way of providing the necessary care and medical treatment that the patient requires[7]. Although the nearest relative may make an application under the MHA, usually the social worker is the appropriate person. If the social worker makes an application under section 2 he must consult with the nearest relative beforehand or as soon as possible. The nearest relative must also be contacted before a section 3 application is made (unless it is impracticable or would cause unreasonable delay) and the application cannot go ahead if the nearest relative objects, although, as stated above, a court does have the power to replace the nearest relative if, for example, it is thought that he or she is objecting unreasonably.

The doctors

In the circumstances where two doctors are required to make recommendations under the MHA, at least one of them must have been approved under section 12. This means that they must have met certain criteria and will have received approval from a Health Authority to carry out the various functions under the MHA. If the approved doctor does not know the patient then the other doctor should have known the patient beforehand (e.g. be his general practitioner), but there is no legal requirement for the second doctor to be approved under section 12. If it is not possible to have a doctor who knows the patient, the application may still be made, although the Code of Practice recommends that both doctors are approved under section 12 in these circumstances. The two doctors must be independent of each other in terms of their professional relationship. They must also be independent of the person making the application and of the patient. For example, the patient's brother-in-law cannot provide one of the medical recommendations.

Although there is an exception in an emergency, in the case of an NHS patient only one of the medical recommendations may come from a doctor on the staff of the hospital to which the patient is being admitted. In the case of a private patient being admitted to an NHS hospital or any patient admitted to a mental nursing home, neither recommendation can come from a doctor on the staff. A doctor who has a financial interest (direct or indirect) in a mental nursing home/hospital cannot provide one of the recommendations and neither can his relatives, colleagues or employees. However, the Code of Practice (para. 2.30) makes it clear that it is acceptable for one of the two doctors making the medical recommendations to be on the staff of one hospital and the second doctor to be on the staff of another hospital, even if they are managed by the same NHS Trust, as long as the hospitals are at different locations and have different names.

Section 2: admission for assessment

The requirements that have to be met for a patient to be compulsorily admitted using this section are:

1. A mental disorder which justifies detention.
2. The detention is for assessment (followed by treatment if necessary).
3. It is in the interests of the patient's own health (physical or mental) and safety or with a view to the protection of other persons (one person in danger would be enough).

The period of detention includes the day of admission and only lasts for a maximum of 28 days. The period cannot be renewed and continued detention must rely on the use of another section of the MHA.

The definition of mental disorder is very wide in the MHA and, therefore, no further classification of the illness is necessary for detention under section 2. The definition is 'mental illness, arrested or incomplete development of mind, psychopathic disorder and any other disorder or disability of mind' (section 1(2)).

For example, a suicidal patient may present with apparent depression but have features that suggest a personality disorder as an alternative diagnosis. For the purposes of section 2 the difference in diagnosis is not relevant as long as the other criteria are met.

Section 3: admission for treatment

The requirements for compulsory admission under this section are as outlined below.

1. The patient is suffering from:
   (a) mental illness, or
   (b) severe mental impairment, or
   (c) psychopathic disorder, or
   (d) mental impairment
   and this mental disorder (i.e. a, b, c or d above) makes it appropriate for him to receive medical treatment in a hospital.
2. The detention is necessary (i.e. there is no appropriate alternative) for the health of the patient and/or the protection of other persons.
3. The treatment is necessary and it cannot be provided unless the patient is detained under section 3.

Furthermore, in the case of psychopathic disorder and mental impairment the treatment must be likely to alleviate or prevent a deterioration in the patient's condition (i.e. it is not allowed as a form of imprisonment when there is no benefit to the patient).

The period of detention under section 3 is up to 6 months. The responsible medical officer (i.e. the doctor ultimately in charge of the patient's treatment, who will usually be a consultant) must assess the patient during the 2 months before the detention period expires and decide if renewed detention is necessary according to the criteria set out in the MHA[8]. Detention can then be renewed for a further 6 months. At the next renewal the period is 1 year and remains so from then on.

Unlike for section 2, the patient's mental disorder must be within one of the four categories mentioned. Mental illness is not defined in the Act and is a matter of clinical judgement. This is the category for the majority of cases of admission and includes, for example, schizophrenia and depression. The other three categories are defined in section 1(2) as follows:

- Severe mental impairment: 'A state of arrested or incomplete development of mind which includes severe impairment of intelligence and social functioning and is associated with abnormally aggressive or seriously irresponsible conduct on the part of the person concerned.'

- Mental impairment: 'A state of arrested or incomplete development of mind (not amounting to severe mental impairment) which includes significant impairment of intelligence and social functioning and is associated with abnormally aggressive or seriously irresponsible conduct on the part of the person concerned.'
- Psychopathic disorder: 'A persistent disorder or disability of mind (whether or not including significant impairment of intelligence) which results in abnormally aggressive or seriously irresponsible conduct on the part of the person concerned.'

The term 'mental impairment' refers to people with learning disabilities whose mental abilities have never fully developed. It does not include patients who have suffered an injury or illness which results in the loss of mental function once it has already developed. The various features required in the definition are a matter of clinical judgement after careful analysis. It is important to note that promiscuity or other immoral conduct, sexual deviancy and dependency on alcohol or drugs by themselves are specifically excluded by section 1(3) from the definitions of mental disorder and the other definitions in section 1(2).

Informal patients

Of course, there is no need for compulsory powers of detention to be used if the patient will agree to being admitted and consents to treatment. However, some patients may not have the necessary mental capacity to consent to treatment. Furthermore, their mental condition may mean that they do not either verbally or physically resist admission or treatment. There has been a debate over whether such patients should be detained under the MHA, as failing to do so means they do not have the benefit of the safeguards of patients' rights. The House of Lords in the case of R v Bournewood Community and Mental Health NHS Trust[9] decided that such patients did not have to be detained under the MHA and could be admitted and treated if it is in their best interests (see Chapters 5 and 6).

The emergency situation

In an urgent situation there may be little time to comply with the formalities of an application under sections 2 or 3. Indeed, in a general hospital the necessary staff may not be present. There are, however, lawful ways of detaining and treating patients in emergencies under certain circumstances. These are detailed below.

Under the common law

The common law makes it lawful for anyone to detain someone who is mentally disordered if it is necessary to protect that person and others from harm. Any person making such a decision would need to be able to justify their decision by showing that the person was mentally disordered and that the detention was necessary.

For example, a casualty officer may have assessed a patient as being acutely suicidal and suffering from depression. It would be lawful to use the minimum reasonable force necessary to keep the patient in the department until an urgent psychiatric assessment could take place. In fact, if a patient without mental capacity was allowed to leave and came to harm there is a potential claim for damages.

The in-patient

Section 5(2) of the MHA allows the detention of an in-patient for 72 hours if it appears to the doctor in charge of his/her treatment that he or she ought to be detained under section 2 or section 3. The 'doctor in charge' is either the consultant under whom the patient has been admitted or his or her nominated deputy. It is advisable to have a nominated deputy as a matter of routine as once an emergency has arisen there is unlikely to be time to organize the necessary formalities. The 72 hour period starts when a report (form 12) is sent to the hospital managers. This power does not allow detention of a patient who is already on a section 2 or 3 and applies only to informal patients (i.e. they have agreed to be admitted). However, it can be used to detain a patient being treated for a physical illness if it appears that a section 2 or 3 application ought to be made and the doctor should make immediate contact with a psychiatrist (Code of Practice para. 8.5). Once invoked, the process for a section 2 or 3 application should be started.

Certain classes of registered nurse who care for the mentally ill and mentally handicapped also have the power to detain a patient for up to 6 hours under section 5(4) of the MHA. The nurse can act if a doctor is not immediately available for a section 5(2) and the patient is receiving treatment and is suffering from mental disorder (see definition above) to such a degree that it is necessary for his health and safety or for the protection of others for him to be immediately restrained from leaving the hospital.

No time for a full section 2

In cases of a real emergency ('urgent necessity') when a second doctor cannot be found, section 4 of the MHA allows a section 2 application to proceed on the basis of the report of one doctor. In these circumstances the detention only lasts for 72 hours but it can be converted to a section 2 on receipt of a second medical report (within the 72 hour period) or alternatively a section 3 application can be made.

The powers of the police in an emergency

The police have the power under section 136 of the MHA to remove from a public place a person who appears to be suffering from a mental disorder if the person is in immediate need of care and control. The person must be taken to a place of safety[10], usually a hospital although it may be a police station. The removal must be 'in the interests of that person or for the protection of other persons' and it should be noted that the protection of property is not included. The person must be assessed by a doctor and an approved social worker as soon as possible and they may be detained for a period of up to 72 hours for that purpose.

Safeguards

The MHA has procedures to safeguard the patients detained under the Act. These are summarized below:

1. The powers of the nearest relative.
2. The procedures in the Act itself.
3. The Mental Health Review Tribunal.

The patient is also able to take legal action in the form of:

1. An action for habeas corpus.
2. Judicial review.

The nearest relative can prevent a patient's admission under section 3 by objecting to it and may also discharge a patient from a section 2 or 3 by first giving 72 hours' notice in writing. However, both of these powers may be overcome using procedures in the MHA to safeguard the patient from action by the nearest relative on the basis that, if discharged, the patient would be likely to act in a manner dangerous to other persons or to himself[11].

The MHA also created the Mental Health Review Tribunals. These tribunals are made up of medical and non-medical members with a power to discharge detained patients on review of their case. The applications for review may be made by the patient and/or the nearest relative depending on the power under which the patient is detained. There is also provision for automatic review of some cases, for example patients detained under section 3 if they have not made an application themselves within certain time periods. The detaining authority has a duty to start this process.

A patient is also able to use the general law to oppose any detention. A writ of habeas corpus can be issued alleging that the detention is unlawful. The court can also be asked to review any administrative decision and this is known as judicial review. For example, although a detention under the MHA appears lawful, a judge may be asked to find that the decision making process was at fault for some reason, perhaps because it was unreasonable (for example, an inadequate medical examination) or a misapplication of the law (for example, a social worker makes an error over the identity of the nearest relative).

Limitations on the power to treat

Once a patient has been appropriately detained they can be given treatment for their mental disorder against their will (but emergency detentions under sections 4, 5(2), 5(4) and 136 are amongst the exclusions). However, for those patients detained under certain sections, including 2 and 3, the consent of the patient *or* a second opinion is required to treat the mental disorder by electroconvulsive therapy (at any time) or to continue any medicine for longer than 3 months (section 58). Certain controversial treatments such as psychosurgery require a second opinion *and* the patient's consent whether they are detained or an informal patient (section 57). However, in an emergency, those consents or opinions may not have to be obtained if various factors are met, one of which is that it 'is immediately necessary to save the patient's life' (section 62).

Treatment of physical conditions

The MHA cannot be used to sanction the compulsory treatment of physical conditions from which a patient suffers, even if the patient is mentally disordered. The process of obtaining a patient's consent should be dealt with in the usual way and if a patient does not have the mental capacity to consent then treatment will only be lawful if it is in the patient's best interests (see Chapters 5 and 6). Section 63 of the MHA allows medical treatment without consent for the mental disorder from which the patient is suffering if detained under certain sections of the MHA including sections 2 and 3 (amongst others, the emergency detentions of sections 4, 5(2) and 5(4) are excluded). The court has decided that medical treatment in section 63 includes alleviating the consequences of and relieving the symptoms of the mental disorder. For example, in the case of a girl with an eating disorder the court held that nasogastric feeding was lawful under section 63 as it was to treat a symptom of the mental disorder[12]. Therefore, for those patients who are appropriately detained, treatment may be given lawfully without consent if it is directed at the symptoms of the mental disorder provided it is under the direction of the consultant in charge of the patient (the responsible medical officer). Obviously, careful consideration would need to be given to whether any proposed treatment comes within this provision and appropriate advice taken beforehand.

Other powers in the MHA

The MHA covers other areas of the treatment and management of property and affairs of the mentally disordered. These include:

1. The provision of a guardian to ensure out-patient treatment.
2. The requirement for, and provision of, supervision for a person after discharge.
3. Provisions for patients concerned in criminal proceedings or under sentence.
4. Transfer of patients.
5. Management of property and affairs of patients.

Summary

The MHA allows for the compulsory detention, assessment and treatment of mentally disordered patients. It also provides safeguards to prevent abuse of these powers. Urgent treatment may be lawful under the common law if it is necessary and the emergency provisions of the MHA cannot be used.

References

1 Department of Health and Welsh Office (1999) *Mental Health Act 1983 Code of Practice*. The Stationery Office
2 Mental Health Act 1983, section 12
3 Mental Health Act 1983, section 26
4 Mental Health (Hospital, Guardianship and Consent to Treatment) Regulations 1983, Regulation 14

5 Mental Health Act 1983, section 29
6 Mental Health Act 1983, section 13
7 Mental Health Act 1983, section 13(2)
8 Mental Health Act 1983, sections 20(1) and (2)
9 [1998] 3 All ER 289
10 Mental Health Act 1983, section 135: definition of a place of safety
11 Mental Health Act 1983, section 25(1)
12 B v Croydon Health Authority [1995] 1 All ER 683. (For further information on treating anorexia nervosa see the Mental Health Act Commission's Guidance Note 3.)

Confidentiality

Patients tell those caring for them a large amount of information that they would not disclose in any other circumstance. This type of information is required in order to make a diagnosis and to treat the patient effectively. In order to feel able to provide this information, the patient must know that it will not be disclosed. A requirement to maintain patient confidentiality is placed on health care professionals in various ways, as listed below.

1. A legal duty: the clinician–patient relationship is one that gives rise to a duty of confidence.
2. By the regulatory bodies of their profession, e.g. the General Medical Council (GMC).
3. By a contract of employment with a health care provider.

What is confidential information?

Any information that has been provided within the confidential relationship will be subject to a duty of confidence and this would, therefore, include the patient's name, address and other personal details as well as clinical information. For example, a telephone call is received on the ward asking if Mr X is a patient. The nurse taking the call states that Mr X is a patient but she cannot let the caller know any treatment details. There has been a potential breach of confidentiality because it has been confirmed that Mr X is in hospital.

Release of confidential information

The patient, of course, may allow the disclosure of confidential information by giving their consent to its release. In order to give consent, the patient must have the necessary mental capacity (see Chapters 5 and 6) and be aware of the circumstances and purpose of the release. On the ward, for example, when informing a relative of a patient's condition it may not be practical or necessary to obtain the written consent of the patient prior to the discussion. In other situations it is advisable to have recorded the agreement to disclosure in writing so that the patient's consent may be demonstrated at a later date if necessary. It is dangerous to assume in all situations that a patient would want information to be passed to a relative without their permission. If a patient is not able to agree then a disclosure should only be made when it is in their best interests.

There are certain circumstances where confidential information may, or even must, be released without the consent of the patient. These situations come under two categories: (1) when it is required by law and (2) in circumstances that are justifiable as being in the public interest.

When release of information is required by law

Examples of this are as follows:

- Notifiable diseases must be reported under the Public Health (Control of Disease) Act 1984.
- In some road traffic offences, information about the identity of the driver must be provided if a request is made by the Chief Officer of Police. In this case the police should make it clear that they are making the request under section 172 of the Road Traffic Act 1988 so that the clinicians are in no doubt as to their obligation.
- The Prevention of Terrorism Act 1989 makes it a criminal offence for a person to fail to provide information about terrorist offences relating to the situation in Northern Ireland.
- In response to a court order. The civil and criminal courts have powers to force a person who has confidential information to disclose it. Failure to obey a court order is contempt and a serious offence. The order may be obtained by requiring a person's attendance at court, where a judge will make the order orally. In the absence of any attendance at court, information should not be released unless a verifiable written order of the court, which has been sealed, is provided. It would be inadvisable to rely on an assurance that disclosure must be given.

To illustrate the final point above, consider a driver being sued by a pedestrian for damages after a road traffic accident. The solicitor acting for the driver telephoned the pedestrian's doctor and asked for copies of the medical records. The doctor was told that he could be forced to release the records by court order so he might as well give them up voluntarily.

In the absence of the patient's consent, disclosure by the doctor in these circumstances would be a breach of confidentiality. An appropriate response would be to ask the solicitor to obtain the patient's consent in writing or to provide a court order requiring the release. This would absolve the doctor from the breach of confidentiality.

When release of information is justifiable as being in the public interest

There are circumstances in which the public interest of keeping medical information confidential is outweighed by another public interest. The 'public interest' is a technical term and is a justification used to make lawful certain acts which benefit the public although they may breach an individual's rights. There is no precise definition of which disclosures are in the public interest and it depends on the circumstances. However, it is likely that disclosure of information concerning a serious crime would be found to be in the public interest. There is no definition of what amounts to a serious crime in this context but it is generally accepted that an offence which is defined as a 'serious arrestable offence' in the Police and Criminal Evidence Act 1984 would be considered 'serious' for these purposes. These offences include murder, manslaughter, rape, serious assault, certain sexual offences, offences involving children and drug offences.

The GMC's guidance on confidentiality[1] states:

'Disclosures may be necessary in the public interest where a failure to disclose information may expose the patient, or others, to risk of death or serious harm. In such circumstances you should disclose information promptly to an appropriate person or authority.'

The guidance goes on to use as examples a patient who carries on driving against medical advice, a doctor who places patients at risk due to his own medical condition and the prevention or detection of a serious crime.

For example, a doctor was commissioned by a patient detained under the Mental Health Act to prepare a report to be used in an application to review his detention. The patient had been detained after he had shot several people and used explosive devices. The doctor's assessment was not favourable to the patient and did not agree with the treating doctor's assessment and the application did not proceed. The doctor's opinion was that his report should be disclosed to the doctors looking after the patient because, in his view, important matters relating to the dangerousness of the patient had not been explored. The doctor released the report and the patient sued for breach of confidentiality and to have the report returned. The court held that the balance of public interests (i.e. confidentiality against public safety) was in favour of disclosure because of the seriousness of the offences that the patient had committed and the need for the authorities to have relevant information about his medical condition before making decisions that might lead to his release[2].

Requests by the police for information

It is common for the police to request confidential information when they are investigating an offence, either about a potential defendant or the victim of a crime. In the absence of the patient's consent it may be possible to say that, on the face of it, disclosure would be justified on the basis of a serious crime having been committed (see above), but further matters need to be considered before disclosure is undertaken:

1. Is disclosure absolutely necessary? Before releasing information it should be established that the release of information is needed by the police to advance their investigation. For example, the request may be a matter of routine and do they in fact have enough evidence? The police should be asked to justify their request in writing.
2. What is the minimum information that is required? There is no need to disclose all of the patient's medical records if only a certain part of them would be sufficient. Ask the police to justify their request.
3. Does the information relate to a particular patient? Occasionally the police may make a request for information that relates to a group of patients. For example, all patients who attended A&E and had a cut hand or all patients on leave from a psychiatric hospital on a particular day. It is highly unlikely that the release of a series of patients' records in this type of circumstance would be justifiable as being in the public interest.

The Department of Health guidance[3] states:

'Passing on information to help tackle serious crime. . .may be justified if the following conditions are satisfied:

1. without disclosure, the task of preventing, detecting or prosecuting the crime would be seriously prejudiced or delayed;
2. information is limited to what is strictly relevant to a specific investigation;
3. there are satisfactory undertakings that the information will not be passed on or used for any purpose other than the present investigation.'

Children

The duty of confidentiality to people below the age of eighteen years follows the principles applied to obtaining their consent to treatment. A child of sixteen years or above should be treated in the same way as an adult. Those children below sixteen years should have their confidence respected if they have sufficient intelligence to understand the nature and effect of their treatment including the risks and benefits[4]. However, the child should always be encouraged and counselled to allow the parents to be informed. For example, in the well-known Gillick case it was decided that a child under sixteen years of age who requests contraceptives may be given that treatment without the knowledge or consent of her parents if she has sufficient intelligence and understanding of the nature of the proposed treatment. The child should be encouraged to involve her parents.

Passing information between health care professionals

Information has to be passed between those directly caring for the patient and others such as social workers. When a patient changes general practitioner their notes are passed from one practice to another. If the patient specifically prohibits the passage of information then that should be observed unless, perhaps, disclosure would be justifiable (see above). A patient should be clearly told of any difficulties that might occur in their treatment as a consequence of that refusal. The GMC and NHS require staff to see that patients are informed about the passage of confidential information. Neither the NHS nor the GMC requires the patient's explicit consent to passage of information within a team (the Department of Health guidance[3] uses the phrase 'for NHS purposes on a need to know basis', which is probably wider). The GMC guidance[1] states:

> 'Where disclosure of relevant information between health care professionals is clearly required for treatment to which a patient has agreed, the patient's explicit consent may not be required. For example, explicit consent would not be needed where a general practitioner discloses relevant information to a medical secretary to have a referral letter typed or a physician makes relevant information available to a radiologist when requesting an X-ray.'

Summary

Information provided by patients must be kept confidential unless they have given their consent to its release. There are situations when the duty of confidence may be breached because of an obligation imposed by the law or where there are justifiable circumstances.

References

1 General Medical Council (1995) *Confidentiality Guidance from the General Medical Council*
2 W v Egdell [1990] 1 All ER 835
3 Department of Health (1996) *The Protection and Use of Patient Information*. HMSO
4 Gillick v West Norfolk Health Authority [1985] 3 All ER 402

10

The coroner's inquest

The office of coroner is an extremely old one going back around 800 years. However, over that time the coroner's functions have changed and become more limited. The coroner's powers originally related to protecting the financial interests of the Crown in local affairs and investigating and detaining criminals.

Today, the coroner's role is essentially two-fold: first, to hold inquests into deaths and secondly, to hold inquests into treasure troves. The latter is not within the scope of this book and will not be mentioned further.

When does the coroner become involved?

The coroner is required to hold an inquest into deaths[1] where there is reasonable cause to suspect that the death was:

1. violent or unnatural;
2. sudden and of unknown cause;
3. in prison or elsewhere in circumstances where another Act of Parliament requires an inquest to be held.

Death certificates and reporting cases to the coroner

Every death has to be registered within 5 days with the Registrar of Births, Marriages and Deaths, although there are certain special regulations with regard to ships and aircraft. Any doctor who has attended the deceased during his last illness must fill out a death certificate which states, to the best of his knowledge and belief, the cause of death. The doctor must also give the person who has to register the death (usually a relative) a written notice of the certificate, which identifies the cause of death as detailed on the certificate.

In cases which appear to come within the coroner's jurisdiction (i.e. points 1, 2 or 3 above) a doctor should report them to the coroner's officer. Relatives should be told that the death cannot be registered until the coroner has finished his investigation.

If, for whatever reason, the doctor has not notified the coroner, the Registrar is obliged to do so when[2]:

1. The deceased was not attended by a doctor in his last illness.
2. He is unable to obtain a completed death certificate.
3. The deceased was not seen by the doctor completing the certificate either after death or within 14 days before death.
4. The cause of death is unknown.
5. The death was unnatural or caused by violence or neglect or by abortion or in suspicious circumstances.
6. The death occurred during or within 24 hours of an operation or before recovery from the effects of an anaesthetic.
7. The cause of death was due to an industrial disease or industrial poisoning.

Of course, any death that has been caused by any medical or surgical treatment, or its complications, is, on the face of it, an unnatural death and so should be reported under point 5 above, even if the treatment was given more than 24 hours before death.

In practice, when a patient has died, a doctor should notify the coroner if the case falls within the circumstances above before the Registrar has to do so, for example if the cause of death is unknown or related to surgical or medical treatment.

Coroner's procedure before an inquest

Notification is usually communicated through the coroner's officer, who is usually (but not necessarily) a police officer. The coroner's officer will carry out investigations on behalf of the coroner into the circumstances surrounding the death. On the basis of these investigations the coroner may decide that a post mortem is necessary to help determine if he should hold an inquest. After these investigations the coroner must hold an inquest if he believes the death was violent, unnatural, sudden or of unknown cause or in prison etc.

The inquest

An inquest is unique in the judicial processes of England and Wales as it takes the form of an inquiry by the coroner. Other courts operate on an adversarial system where there are opposing parties, in other words, one party investigates and tries to prove their case and the other defends, with the court resolving the dispute between them. At an inquest there are no parties and no case is presented. It is the coroner's inquiry to determine the facts in order to answer the limited questions that he is required to address.

The coroner hears evidence from the people that he calls, whom he considers can give evidence about the death. A request from the coroner's officer for a written statement may be the first indication that a doctor or other health care professional has that an inquest is going to be held into the death of a patient. It is advisable to seek advice at this early stage, either from a medical defence organization or, in the case of a clinician in a hospital/community setting, from the legal department at his or her employing Trust. The coroner may not have notified the Trust itself of the inquest. If a person's conduct is likely to have caused or contributed to the death, then the coroner should give formal notice of the inquest to that person.

What questions does the inquest address?

The remit of the inquest is limited. The purpose is to answer four factual questions[3]:

1. who the deceased was;
2. how the deceased came by his death;
3. when the deceased came by his death;
4. where the deceased came by his death.

A verdict must not determine any question of criminal liability on the part of any named person or civil liability (i.e. negligence)[4]. If, during the inquest, it appears that criminal homicide is involved, the inquest will have to be adjourned and nobody has to answer any questions that might lead to self-incrimination.

The rules are not as strict for civil liability and the inquest will consider the facts surrounding the death but the questioning should only be relevant to answering the four questions above and the coroner can disallow any other questions. Nevertheless, the coroner may allow the questioning to cover a wide area on the basis that the facts must be fully explored and it may help the relatives of the deceased to come to terms with the death.

The hearing

Coroners' courts vary from rooms in modern buildings to rather more formal surroundings. The inquest may be opened formally by the coroner's officer with a proclamation or simply by asking those present to stand as the coroner enters the room.

The interested parties, if acting in person, or their representatives, usually sit in the front row of seating facing the coroner, with witnesses and members of the public in the other seats. The coroner usually starts by explaining the purpose of the inquest and then calls the first witness, who is usually a member of the family of the deceased. The witnesses then generally follow in chronological order.

As it is an inquiry by the coroner, he asks questions of the witnesses first (which may include expert witnesses) in order to answer the four questions. However, other interested parties are also entitled to ask witnesses questions, either themselves or via a barrister or solicitor. 'Interested parties' include the close relatives of the deceased and anyone who may have caused or contributed to the death. Unlike in a criminal court, all the witnesses (and anyone else attending the inquest) remain in court throughout the hearing or they may leave after giving evidence if they are released by the coroner.

Having heard the evidence the coroner (sometimes after a break) will summarize the evidence and findings of fact and give the verdict. The usual end to the inquest is signalled when all are asked to rise as the coroner leaves.

In certain circumstances the coroner must have a jury to make the findings of fact. The procedure is altered in these circumstances as the jury will have to be sworn in at the beginning and they give the verdict after the coroner has given them directions.

The findings of fact

Who the deceased was, where he or she died and the time of death are usually not controversial but 'how' the deceased came by his death can cause difficulties.

The 'how' referred to is to be taken as meaning 'by what means' and not 'in what circumstances'[5]. There are various possible answers to this part of the verdict, which include:

- natural causes
- industrial disease
- dependence on drugs/non-dependent abuse of drugs
- want of attention at birth
- suicide
- attempted/self-induced abortion
- accident/misadventure
- sentence of death
- lawful killing
- open verdict

- unlawful killing
- stillbirth.

In addition, neglect or self-neglect may rarely be found or, more usually, may qualify the findings.

In cases involving medical care, the question of whether the death was from natural causes or an accident may cause difficulties. Furthermore, the possibility of neglect can be raised and has caused difficulties in previous cases because of its apparent relationship to lack of care in the sense of negligent treatment.

'Natural causes' or 'accident/misadventure'

Although the finding may be of either accident or misadventure, the courts have held that there is no difference between the two terms and accident is the preferred terminology.

When a death has occurred during a course of medical treatment or in the presence of a potentially treatable medical condition it may be hard to determine whether the death was unnatural, i.e. a result of the treatment, or natural, i.e. the result of the disease. For example, death following an operation for a perforated duodenal ulcer may be because of the effects of peritonitis from the disease rather than the effects of the operation itself. A finding of accident/misadventure does not imply fault because it refers to the 'mode' of death, not the surrounding circumstances. Similarly, a finding of natural causes following the operation for a perforated duodenal ulcer does not necessarily mean there was no negligence during the operation.

For example, a two year old boy had breathing problems and a bronchoscopy was recommended. After the bronchoscopy surgical emphysema developed but a decision was made not to insert chest drains. Unfortunately, the child had a cardiac arrest and died. The evidence of the pathologist at the inquest was that the death was due to:

1(a) bilateral tension pneumothorax
1(b) artificial ventilation
1(c) acute tracheobronchitis and bronchiolitis.

The members of the jury at the inquest were told by the coroner that the only verdict was natural causes. The family applied to the court to overturn the verdict. The judge held that, on the one hand, the child had a potentially life-threatening illness of tracheobronchitis and bronchiolitis and treatment had failed to prevent his death. However, on the other hand, the bilateral pneumothoraces, which might have been caused by the investigation and/or the effect of the investigation on the underlying diseased lungs, would not amount to natural causes. He therefore quashed the verdict as the jury should have been allowed to decide between accident/misadventure and natural causes[6].

Neglect

Until recently the phrase 'lack of care' was used to qualify verdicts; for example 'accident/misadventure aggravated by lack of care'. The relatives may have wished to see that phrase used to demonstrate cases where there had been a failure in the care given to the deceased. However, the phrase is meant to mean 'neglect' and not breach of a duty of care owed to a patient. Neglect has been described as meaning 'a gross failure to provide adequate nourishment or liquid or provide or procure basic medical attention or shelter or warmth for someone in a dependant position (because of youth, age, illness or incarceration) who cannot provide it for himself' and as the converse of self-neglect[5]. In order for neglect to be properly part of the verdict there must also be a causal link between the neglect and the death[5].

For example, a twenty-seven year old man was admitted as a day case for removal of his wisdom teeth under a general anaesthetic. During the anaesthetic there must have been an obstruction of his airway and he never regained consciousness and died a few days later.

The inquest was opened and then adjourned as the possibility of criminal charges were investigated. No charges were subsequently brought and so the inquest was recommenced. During the inquest the coroner said that those who had care of the deceased had failed to maintain his airway, which led to the death. The coroner's verdict was accidental death. The relatives of the deceased applied for a new inquest on a variety of grounds but one was that the coroner should have given a verdict of 'lack of care'. The judge did not criticize this part of the coroner's verdict on the basis that, first, 'lack of care' was not the appropriate terminology and, secondly, 'neglect' meant a continuous or at least non-transient neglect and was not an appropriate description of the negligent lack of care which was alleged to have led to the death in this case[7].

Summary

The coroner inquires into the circumstances of a death to answer four limited questions. Nevertheless, an inquest can raise difficult issues over how the deceased came by their death, although the coroner must not make any determination of civil or criminal liability.

References

1 Coroner's Act 1988, section 8
2 Registration of Births and Deaths Regulations 1987/2088
3 Coroner's Act 1988, section 11(5)
4 Coroner's Rules 1984, rule 42
5 R v North Humberside Coroner ex parte Jamieson [1994] 2 All ER 972. Text in quotations copyright Butterworth and Co. (Publishers) Ltd, reproduced by permission of the Butterworths Division of Reed Elsevier (UK) Ltd
6 R v HM Coroner for Birmingham and Solihull exp. Benton [1997] 8 Med LR 362
7 R v Surrey Coroner, ex parte Wright [1997] QB 786

11

The General Medical Council

The medical profession is regulated in the UK by the General Medical Council (GMC). The GMC is constituted according to the law set out in the Medical Act 1983 (the Act). Its purpose is to protect the public from medical practitioners who have not been adequately trained and those who fall short of the standards expected of the profession.

The make-up of the GMC

The majority of the members of the GMC are registered medical practitioners with a minority being non-medical people. The members of the council are made up of:

- Elected members. There are fifty-four doctors elected from four constituencies: England, the Channel Islands and the Isle of Man; Wales; Scotland; and Northern Ireland.
- Appointed members. There are twenty-five doctors selected by the universities, medical schools and other bodies which are able to award medical qualifications that can lead to registration under the Act.
- Nominated members. There are twenty-five non-medically qualified individuals who are nominated by the Privy Council to sit on the GMC.

From amongst the members of the GMC a President is elected and the Council appoints a Registrar to ensure that the registers are up to date as specified under the Act. There are also six committees to carry out the regulatory functions required under the Act. These are:

- the Preliminary Proceedings Committee
- the Professional Conduct Committee
- the Health Committee
- the Education Committee
- the Assessment Referral Committee
- the Committee on Professional Performance.

The functions of the GMC

The GMC is a regulatory body with the motto 'protecting patients, guiding doctors'. The GMC carries out its role by:

1. Being responsible for the standards of medical education.
2. Keeping a register of doctors.
3. Having the power to remove or suspend registration or put conditions on a doctor's practice.
4. Advising doctors on the standards of professional conduct and on medical ethics.

Standards in medical education

The Education Committee must promote high standards and co-ordinate all stages of medical education[1]. This committee must produce recommendations for the various bodies that are able to award medical qualifications, having determined the extent of knowledge and skill and standards of proficiency required. It is also responsible for setting the required experience to be obtained in the pre-registration house officer year.

The committee monitors the bodies that award qualifications by a process of inspections and visitations. The ultimate sanction open to the committee is to recommend to the Privy Council that the qualification in question is no longer recognized under the Act as one that entitles the holder to be registered.

Keeping a register of doctors

In order to practice medicine lawfully a doctor must be registered with the GMC. The GMC has to keep a register of these practitioners and this is published annually in paper form and is also available on the Internet. Also, anyone may telephone the GMC to enquire about a doctor's registration. The openness of the register means that people are able to check that the person they are being treated by, or are intending to employ, is registered as a doctor and will therefore have met certain standards.

There are different types of registration: provisional, full and limited. Attaining an appropriate qualification as a doctor does not automatically allow for full registration, as a year of clinical experience has to be undertaken at an approved hospital. During this time the doctor is given provisional registration. To overcome the restrictions that only allow fully registered practitioners to carry out certain tasks, the provisionally registered doctor is treated as fully registered so far as is necessary to enable him to be employed[2]. For example, a house officer may lawfully prescribe a prescription-only medicine in the context of his job as a house officer but not in any other circumstance.

In addition to the degrees awarded by university medical schools, an individual is entitled to registration if they are awarded licentiates from the Royal Colleges of Physicians and Surgeons or a licentiate in medicine from the Society of Apothecaries of London[3]. Furthermore, a national of any European Economic Area state with an appropriate medical qualification and certain people who have qualified outside these areas are entitled to be registered in the UK[4].

Limited registration can be given to those who are not entitled to full registration. In order to obtain this type of registration the individual must hold an acceptable qualification and have been selected for employment at an approved hospital in the UK or Isle of Man. Furthermore, the Registrar must be satisfied that he or she has the necessary knowledge of English (unless exempt), is of good character and has the required skill, knowledge and experience[5]. A doctor can only hold limited registration for 5 years. It allows the doctor to practice under supervision and only in a limited capacity, for example in a particular speciality. The details of the limitation of those practitioners with limited registration are available on the register. Again, in order to carry out their job, a person with limited registration is treated as being fully registered.

The power to affect a doctor's registration

The GMC has the power to affect a doctor's registration in the following circumstances:

1. When the doctor has been convicted of a criminal offence[6].
2. When it is judged that he or she has been guilty of serious professional misconduct[6].
3. When the doctor's fitness to practise is judged to be seriously impaired by reason of his or her physical or mental condition[7].
4. When the doctor's professional performance has been found to be seriously deficient[8].

Conviction for a criminal offence

The police and courts will report doctors who have been convicted of criminal offences to the GMC. It is not possible for a practitioner to argue before the GMC that they are innocent of the crime if they have been convicted of it in a court. Therefore, any submissions that are made will concentrate on why the conviction should not be allowed to affect the doctor's registration. The matter will be dealt with by the Preliminary Proceedings committee and, if serious, it will be referred to the Professional Conduct Committee (see below for details of the procedures)[9].

Serious professional misconduct

In its publications the GMC refers to serious professional misconduct as being '...behaviour which calls into question whether a doctor should be allowed to continue to practise medicine without restriction'[10] and where a doctor's conduct '...falls seriously short of accepted standards'[9]. The court has stated that misconduct involves some act or omission which falls short of what would be proper in the circumstances[11] and that serious professional misconduct is conduct that no doctor of reasonable skill, exercising reasonable care, would carry out[12].

In order to determine the standards to be expected of the doctor, regard will be given to the GMC publication *Good Medical Practice*[13] and doctors should be familiar with its content and that of other GMC publications regarding, for example, consent and confidentiality[14,15]. Examples provided by the GMC of conduct that could lead to a finding of professional misconduct are[16]:

1. Serious neglect or disregard of professional responsibilities to patients.
2. Certifying as true, information which the doctor knows to be untrue or has not taken appropriate steps to verify.
3. Improper charging of private fees to NHS patients or false claims on the NHS.
4. Any other form of dishonesty.
5. Any abuse by the doctor of their position of trust, including a breach of professional confidence.
6. Any form of indecency or inappropriate sexual conduct towards a patient or colleague or any other person.

Serious professional misconduct could be found in cases where the treatment was seriously negligent, although it is unlikely that an individual negligent act would result in such a finding. In the case of McCandless v GMC[12] the court upheld the GMC's finding of serious professional misconduct against a doctor. It was alleged that he had made three errors in the diagnoses of three patients and failed to refer them to hospital and two of the patients had later died. The doctor argued that as these where honest mistakes he should not be guilty of serious professional misconduct. The court agreed with the GMC that care which had fallen deplorably short of the standard which patients were entitled to expect could amount to serious professional misconduct.

A finding of serious professional misconduct might also occur even if the doctor is not directly treating patients if the behaviour is bad enough. Furthermore, if there is a sufficiently close link, the general obligation to care for the sick might co-exist with another duty and therefore lead to a finding of serious professional misconduct even if the doctor's predominant occupation was not direct patient care. For example, the Chief Executive of a Trust was also a consultant radiologist. Serious concerns arose about the mortality of children undergoing paediatric cardiac surgery under the care of other consultants at the Trust. The GMC found the radiologist guilty of serious professional misconduct in that he had failed to take action over the years when concerns were raised and there had been a failure to cancel a child's operation (the child died later). It had been argued on the doctor's behalf that he should not have been found guilty by the GMC as he was acting as the Chief Executive and not a doctor. The court upheld the GMC's finding on the basis that the duty to care for the sick co-existed with the duty to protect patients as Chief Executive, and that there was a sufficiently close link between the profession of medicine and the post of Chief Executive of the Trust for such a finding to have been properly made[11].

Mental and physical health

If a doctor's practice is seriously affected by ill health then the GMC will investigate and may remove the practitioner's registration or put conditions on his or her practice in order to protect patients. The GMC has stated that most of the referrals are for mental illness and alcohol or drug abuse[17].

Professional performance

Seriously deficient professional performance may lead to a doctor's registration being suspended or conditions being imposed on his or her practice. The GMC has defined seriously deficient performance as 'a departure from good practice, whether or not it is covered by specific GMC guidance, sufficiently serious to call into question a doctor's registration'. They go on to state the following[18]: 'This means that [the GMC] will question [the doctor's] registration if [the GMC] believe that [the doctor is], repeatedly or persistently, not meeting the professional standards appropriate to the work that [the doctor is] doing—especially if [the doctor] might be putting patients at risk. This could include failure to follow the guidance in [the GMC's] booklet *Good Medical Practice*.'[18]

Examples given by the GMC of problems with performance are[16]:

1. Failure to keep professional knowledge and skills up to date.
2. Failure to recognize the limits of professional competence.

3. Failure to maintain any or adequate clinical records.
4. Inability or unwillingness to take an adequate history or to perform a competent physical examination.
5. Attempting to practise techniques in which the doctor has not been appropriately trained.
6. Inability or refusal to communicate effectively with patients or their relatives.
7. Failure to work effectively with colleagues.

The GMC has stated that the procedures are not meant to look into individual incidents[16]. However, an individual incident may indicate an underlying problem of performance which is likely to lead to an investigation.

The process of a complaint

The procedures of the GMC are complex. Anyone who becomes subject to an investigation by the GMC should take advice from their medical defence organization or independent legal advice. The following is a summary of the process of a complaint.

Anyone may make a complaint to the GMC. It may be a member of the public or another doctor or the employer, NHS Trust or Health Authority. The initial process for the investigation is similar whatever conduct is the subject of the complaint.

The complaint is dealt with by a medically qualified screener who decides if there is a case to answer under the grounds of conduct, professional performance or health. In a complaint about conduct or professional performance, if the medical screener does not believe that there is a problem it will be referred for the opinion of a non-medically qualified screener. If both screeners are in agreement, then the case will not proceed. Thereafter the processes are different.

Health

A screener may decide that no action is necessary if the problem is being resolved by steps that have already been taken informally. However, further action will mean the doctor is asked to undergo a medical examination by two doctors with relevant experience. These doctors address the question of whether the ability to practise has been seriously impaired and may make recommendations limiting the doctor's practice. If the doctor co-operates then the matter is dealt with in this way. However, failure to co-operate results in the case coming before the Health Committee. This committee meets in private and has seven medical members and two non-medical members of the GMC. At the hearing of the committee the doctor may have representation. When it gives its decision the Health Committee should briefly set out the reasons underlying it[19].

If the Health Committee finds that the ability to practise is seriously impaired by ill health, then it may suspend the doctor's registration for 12 months or impose conditions on his or her practice for up to 3 years. These can be reviewed at intervals and renewed, or suspension may be converted to registration with conditions. If a person's registration has been suspended for 2 years, the committee may make it indefinite at that point. The practitioner may apply after 2 years and at 2 yearly intervals thereafter to have the suspension lifted[7].

The doctor may appeal to the Privy Council, although such an appeal is limited to a question of law only and not of fact.

Conduct

If further action is required then the case is referred by the screener to the Preliminary Proceedings Committee. This committee may decide that no further action is required or may refer the case to the Professional Conduct Committee for a full hearing. The committee may, however, decide in appropriate cases to send the doctor a letter of advice or warning only. If it appears to the committee that the case is one that is really appropriate for the Health Committee, then they may make a referral to that committee[9,20].

If the case proceeds, then there will be a full hearing in public of the Professional Conduct Committee. The GMC instructs lawyers to investigate and present the case to the committee. The doctor may also be legally represented at the hearing. The proceedings are similar to those of a criminal trial and the facts have to be proved beyond all reasonable doubt.

If this committee finds serious professional misconduct then it may[6]:

1. Erase the doctor from the register. However, after a period of 10 months the doctor can apply to be put back on the register.
2. Suspend a doctor's registration for up to 12 months.
3. Make registration subject to conditions, such as limiting areas of work. This may last for up to 3 years.
4. Admonish the doctor.

A doctor who is suspended may have the suspension renewed for up to 12 months at a time. Furthermore, the suspension can be converted to erasure or conditional registration (again with a 3 year time limit). A conditional registration may be renewed for 12 months or revoked in whole or part.

The doctor may appeal a decision of the committee to the Privy Council.

Professional performance

If the screener decides that further action is required, then the doctor is invited to undergo an assessment of their performance which usually is carried out by two specialists in the relevant area of medicine and a non-medical person. The process is dealt with by a case co-ordinator. Not co-operating at this stage will mean referral to the Assessment Referral Committee who will either decide that there is no case to answer or will order compliance with an assessment. Failure to comply here will result in referral to the Committee on Professional Performance. This committee will decide if there is a case to answer. If there is, then they will order an assessment and a failure to comply could lead to conditions on registration or suspension of registration.

If deficiencies are identified after an assessment, the co-ordinator may decide that the case can be dealt with on a voluntary basis, with the doctor agreeing to restrictions on their practice and to undertaking remedial action. However, if the case is serious, or the doctor does not agree, then the matter is referred to the Committee on Professional Performance.

If the doctor has agreed to take corrective steps, then there will be a reassessment after the training or other action. If the performance is satisfactory the case will be discharged but if not further training may be undertaken if this is likely to be useful. In other cases the matter will be referred to the Committee on Professional Performance.

The hearing of the Committee on Professional Performance is in private and the doctor may have legal representation. The GMC will instruct lawyers to present the case and witnesses and other evidence will be called. The Committee on Professional Performance can impose conditions on a doctor's registration for 3 years or can suspend it for 12 months. Failure to comply with conditions may result in a suspension. A suspension may be converted to conditional registration for a maximum period of 3 years. Any suspension can be made indefinite after a 2 year period. Such a move is reviewed on the doctor's request after 2 years and at 2 yearly intervals thereafter.

There is a right of appeal on a question of law to the Privy Council.

Advice from the GMC on ethics and other matters

The GMC produces various publications (such as the *Good Medical Practice* booklet already referred to) and advice on confidentiality. The contents of these books are not the law but they do reflect the current law and set out the professional rules of practice, which may be more restrictive than the law. For example, a doctor does not owe a legal duty to be candid to a person who is not being treated as his or her patient—such as the parents of a child[21]. However, when something has gone wrong, the GMC has imposed a professional duty on a doctor to explain the situation honestly to those with parental responsibility for an under-sixteen year old (who is not 'Gillick' competent)[22].

Furthermore, the opinions of the GMC are very likely to amount to a responsible body of medical opinion and, therefore, any deviation from standards which have been set may be difficult to defend in any negligence action (see Chapter 3). The courts do take account of the GMC publications and, for this reason and for reasons of professional conduct, doctors should be familiar with the booklets and other statements made by the GMC.

Summary

The GMC is the regulatory body for the medical profession. No doctor may lawfully practise medicine unless they are registered with the GMC. The GMC has the power to erase or suspend a doctor's registration or to impose restrictions on his or her practice if that is necessary. The grounds for these sanctions are serious professional misconduct, seriously deficient professional performance or because the doctor's health has seriously impaired their fitness to practise.

References

1 Medical Act 1983, section 5
2 Medical Act 1983, sections 15, 21 and 55
3 Medical Act 1983, section 4
4 Medical Act 1983, section 3
5 Medical Act 1983, section 22
6 Medical Act 1983, section 36
7 Medical Act 1983, section 37
8 Medical Act 1983, section 36A
9 General Medical Council (1997) *Facing a Complaint—The GMC's Conduct Procedures*
10 General Medical Council (1997) *A Problem With Your Doctor?—How The GMC Deals With Complaints*
11 Roylance v GMC [1999] Lloyds Rep Med 139
12 McCandless v GMC [1996] 7 Med LR 379
13 General Medical Council (1998) *Good Medical Practice*
14 General Medical Council (1998) *Seeking Patients' Consent: The Ethical Considerations*
15 General Medical Council (1995) *Confidentiality—Guidance from the General Medical Council*

16 General Medical Council (1997) *The Management of Doctors with Problems: Referral of Doctors to the GMC's Fitness to Practise Procedures*
17 General Medical Council (1998) *GMC Annual Review*
18 General Medical Council (1997) *When Your Professional Performance is Questioned—The GMC's Performance Procedures*
19 Stefan v GMC [1999] Lloyds Rep Med 90
20 Medical Act 1983, Schedule 4
21 Powell v Boladz [1998] Lloyd's Rep Med 116
22 General Medical Council (1998) *Good Medical Practice*, Paragraph 17

12

Drugs and prescribing

The manufacture, supply and prescription of drugs are heavily controlled by regulations. The principle laws are set out in the Medicines Act 1968 (MA) and the Misuse of Drugs Act 1971 (MDA) and the regulations made under those Acts. The regulatory scheme is based on the premise that nobody is allowed to do anything with a drug unless they have a licence or exemption. Doctors, dentists and pharmacists have wide-ranging exceptions and other health care professionals such as nurses, midwives, health visitors, opticians, ambulance workers and chiropodists have more limited exceptions to allow them to carry on their normal business. In general terms the clinicians act as the gateway for the patient to obtain drugs lawfully.

Classification of drugs

The Medicines Act 1968 classifies medicines into three groups: prescription only medicines (POM), pharmacy medicines (P) and general sales list (GSL).

Prescription only medicines

Medicinal products that are prescription only are listed in schedules to the regulations[1] as are the health professionals who may prescribe them. These drugs can be identified in advertisements and formularies as 'POM' is included in the text. However, POMs include the following classes of products[2]:

1. Controlled drugs (although there are exemptions based on the dose and contents of products).
2. Products for parenteral administration, i.e. administered by breaching the skin or mucous membrane.
3. Those that emit radiation or have the potential to do so.

As a general rule, a POM may not be lawfully given to a patient unless a properly completed prescription has been provided to a pharmacist.

Once a drug has been dispensed by the pharmacist anyone can administer it to anyone else[3] unless it is for parenteral use, when it can only be administered[4]:

1. by the patient to him or herself;
2. by a person entitled to give prescriptions;
3. by a person acting in accordance with the directions of the practitioners in point 2 above.

However, certain substances are excluded from this prohibition if the administration is needed to save life in an emergency[5]. These are:

- adrenaline injection 1 in 1000 (1 mg in 1 ml)
- atropine sulphate injection
- chlorpheniramine injection
- cobalt edetate injection
- dextrose injection strong BPC
- diphenhydramine injection
- glucagon injection
- hydrocortisone injection
- mepyramine injection
- promethazine hydrochloride injection
- snake venom antiserum
- sodium nitrite injection
- sodium thiosulphate injection
- sterile pralidoxime.

Furthermore, a retail pharmacist can give a patient some POMs if certain criteria are fulfilled when a practitioner cannot give a written prescription because of an emergency or a patient requests a POM and the pharmacist is satisfied that there is an immediate need for it[6].

General sales list

A second group of medicinal products are set out in the regulations and are identified by the initials GSL. This means that they may be sold or supplied to patients without a prescription and outside a pharmacy. There are various restrictions, for example, the security of the premises and the packaging of the medicines. This covers, for example, proprietary flu remedies and limited quantities of analgesics, which may be bought in supermarkets.

Pharmacy list

This covers products that are not on the general sales list or prescription only medicines. These are identified by a 'P' and may only be sold or supplied in a retail pharmacy under the ultimate supervision of a pharmacist. Therefore, at large chemist shops, when a product is sold by a salesperson, the pharmacist is always told what product is being supplied.

Exemption to restriction of sale and supply of POM, GSL and P medicines

The restrictions on location and the need for a pharmacist in the sale and supply of POM (although note the prescription is still required), GSL and P medicines do not apply to:

1. Doctors and dentists when they sell or supply to their patient or to another person who is caring for their patient.
2. In a hospital or health centre when the medicine is to be administered in accordance with the directions of a doctor or dentist.

Controlled drugs

Particularly dangerous and addictive drugs are subject to further controls under the Misuse of Drugs Act 1971. These drugs are in three groups: Class A, B or C, and the criminal penalties under the MDA are determined by the class into which the drug falls. Of practical importance to health care staff is the further classification into five schedules. The scope of the restrictions on controlled drugs varies according to which schedule a drug belongs.

- **Schedule 1 drugs**: These are drugs which are deemed to have no medical benefit and therefore any activity associated with the drug is unlawful unless done under a licence. Cannabis is a schedule 1 drug although there is controversy about whether this has properties of therapeutic use. Other schedule 1 drugs include mescaline, cocoa leaf and raw opium.
- **Schedule 2 drugs**: This group contains the well-known opiate drugs used in medicine, such as diamorphine, morphine, codeine and pethidine.
- **Schedule 3 drugs**: Buprenorphine, pentazocine, temazepam and barbiturates are examples of drugs included in this schedule.
- **Schedule 4 drugs**: This group includes hormone preparations and benzodiazepines such as diazepam.
- **Schedule 5 drugs**: The drugs in this section might otherwise be subject to more stringent controls but are at a low concentration or dose (and are not for use by injection), so that the level of control is relaxed. For example, preparations containing no more than 0.1 per cent of cocaine where it cannot be recovered easily or in such an amount as to represent a health risk[7].

Who can do what?

The Misuse of Drugs Act covers the import, export, production, supply, possession and administration of the controlled drugs, including requirements for documentation. The controls for the drugs in schedules 1, 2 and 3 are more comprehensive than those for drugs in schedules 4 and 5.

As would be expected, the MDA covers the activities of conventional medical practice so that they are lawful provided requirements are met. In the community, for example, a GP will issue a prescription (meant for the medical treatment of a single individual) to a patient who will go to a pharmacy. The pharmacy (in lawful possession) will supply the controlled drug on the basis of the prescription. The patient lawfully possesses the drug because it is to be administered for medical purposes in accordance with the directions of his doctor. It would also be lawful for another person to obtain the drug on the patient's behalf and take it to him as it is lawful to possess a controlled drug if it is being taken to another person who may also lawfully possess it.

In the hospital setting the out-patient prescription would be the same as above. For an in-patient where the ward has been supplied by a pharmacist, the sister/charge nurse (or acting sister/charge nurse) in charge of the ward (or theatre or other department) may lawfully possess and supply a controlled drug to a patient for administration to him or her in accordance with the directions of a doctor. If the situation is a hospital or a nursing home where there is no pharmacist responsible for dispensing and supply, then the person in charge (or acting in charge) may lawfully possess and supply to anyone who is entitled to be in lawful possession. For example, a sister in charge of a ward may then supply to the patient on the basis of a prescription by a doctor. This applies to schedule 2, 3, 4 and 5 drugs if the nursing home/hospital is wholly or mainly maintained by public funds or by a charity or voluntary subscriptions (which includes the NHS institutions). Otherwise it only applies to schedule 3 and 4 drugs contained in a medicinal product[8].

There are other people entitled to possess and supply controlled drugs and these include doctors, dentists, midwives and pharmacists when they are acting in those capacities, i.e. it would not be lawful for a doctor to act as a 'drug dealer', as his or her supplying people is only lawful when acting as a doctor.

Prescribing to addicts

A doctor cannot lawfully administer or supply cocaine, diamorphine or dipipanone (or other forms of these drugs) to someone whom he considers, or has reasonable grounds to suspect, is a drug addict unless he holds a special licence or is authorized to do so by the holder of a licence (which is likely to be held by a treatment centre). The exception to this prohibition is if the administration or supply is to treat organic disease or injury. A person is defined as being addicted 'if, and only if, he has, as a result of repeated administration, become so dependent upon the drug that he has an overpowering desire for the administration to be continued'[9].

Administration of a controlled drug

A schedule 5 drug may be administered by anybody to anyone. A schedule 2, 3 or 4 drug may be administered to a patient by a doctor or dentist or by any other person in accordance with the directions of a doctor or dentist. For example, it would not be lawful for a nurse to take from the ward stock a dose of pethidine and administer it to a patient, even if there was a clinical need, without a direction from a doctor or dentist. Such direction will usually be in the form of the chart at the end of the patient's bed.

Midwives and controlled drugs

Appropriately registered midwives are allowed to possess and administer pethidine so far as is necessary for their professional practice. They must surrender any excess stock and have obtained their supply from a specially appointed doctor.

The legal requirements for a prescription

The law requires that a prescription contains various elements. A prescription for a controlled drug in schedule 2 or 3 has more mandatory requirements than other prescriptions.

The requirements for POMs (excluding schedule 2 and 3 drugs) are as follows.

1. The prescriber must sign their name on it in ink.
2. It must be written in ink or another indelible form. It may be written by means of carbon paper or similar material. Computerized prescriptions are therefore lawful (as long as they are actually signed in ink by the prescriber as in 1 above).
3. It must contain the following:
   (a) the address of the prescriber;
   (b) the date of signing or the date before which it is not to be dispensed;
   (c) the prescriber's profession (i.e. doctor, dentist etc.);
   (d) the name, address and age, if under twelve, of the patient.

For a schedule 2 or 3 controlled drug (excluding temazepam) the prescription must:

1. Be written in ink or be otherwise indelible and signed and dated by the prescriber.
2. Be in the prescriber's handwriting and record:
   (a) the name and address of the patient;
   (b) in the case of a preparation, the form (i.e. tablets, elixir etc.), the strength and either the total quantity (in words and figures) or the number of dosage units (in words and figures).
3. The address of the prescriber.

(The above list does not apply for phenobarbitone, where the handwriting requirements in point 2 do not have to be complied with.)

Controlled drug prescriptions are only valid for 13 weeks after the date of issue of the prescription.

In hospital the prescription of a POM does not have to comply with the prescription requirements but it must be a written direction (of course in practice most of the details will be on the drug chart). The prescription of controlled drugs in hospital and/or nursing homes must follow the requirements set out above, except that the requirement for the patient's name and address to be present does not have to be complied with if the prescription is written on the patient's bed card or case sheet.

Who can prescribe?

Prescribing is restricted, in the main, to doctors and dentists. Nurses and health visitors who have attained extra qualifications and been appropriately registered may prescribe a limited number of drugs. These are identified in the British National Formulary in a separate section and are followed by 'NPF' (Nurse Prescribers' Formulary); for example, co-danthramer oral suspension and mebendazole. However, other health care staff, when carrying out their professional practice, are allowed to sell or supply certain drugs that would otherwise be prescription only medicines if certain criteria are fulfilled. For example, a state registered chiropodist who holds an appropriate certificate of competence, in the course of his or her professional practice may sell three days worth (to a maximum of twenty-four tablets) of co-dydramol 10/500 tablets to his/her patient. Other professionals covered by this type of exemption include ambulance workers, ophthalmic opticians and midwives.

Licensed and unlicensed drugs

The Medicines Act controls the processes surrounding medicinal products by the use of licences to permit what would otherwise be unlawful. However, doctors have wide exemptions under the Act and they may prescribe unlicensed products and licensed products for unlicensed indications, which may be lawfully dispensed and supplied to a patient for administration. For example, before an oral preparation of vitamin K was available, the intramuscular preparation was prescribed for oral administration to newborn infants as prophylaxis against haemorrhagic disease of the newborn. The intramuscular preparation was unlicensed for oral administration but there was nothing unlawful in this use because of the exemptions given to doctors.

The prescription of unlicensed drugs or drugs for unlicensed indications may affect the liability of the manufacturer of the drug if there is a defect in the product. However, it will not affect the doctor's liability for any acts or omissions involved in the prescribing or administration of the drug or any defects in obtaining the patient's consent to take the drug. Whether any civil liability to an injured patient exists will be decided on the usual test for medical negligence (see Chapters 3, 5 and 6). Therefore, any use of unlicensed drugs etc. should be capable of being supported by a responsible body of medical opinion, which must withstand logical analysis by a court. In terms of the warnings given when obtaining a patient's consent to treatment with such drugs, it seems likely that the more unusual the drug's use, the more a court would expect a patient to have been fully informed of the consequences and side effects of the treatment.

Summary

All stages involved in the manufacture, supply and prescription of medicinal products are controlled to some degree. The more dangerous the drug, the more stringent the control. Doctors, dentists and pharmacists have very wide exemptions to deal with drugs in the course of their practice, while other health care professionals have more limited exclusions from the controls imposed.

References

1 Prescriptions Only Medicines (Human Use) Order 1997, SI 1997 No. 1830
2 Prescriptions Only Medicines (Human Use) Order 1997, Regulations 3, 5 and 6
3 Prescriptions Only Medicines (Human Use) Order 1997, Regulation 9
4 Medicines Act 1968, section 58(2)(6)
5 Prescriptions Only Medicines (Human Use) Order 1997, Regulation 7

6 Prescriptions Only Medicines (Human Use) Order 1997, Regulation 8
7 Misuse of Drugs Regulations 1985, SI 1985 No. 2066
8 Misuse of Drugs Regulations 1985, Regulation 9
9 Misuse of Drugs (Supply to Addicts) Regulations 1997, SI 1997 No. 1001, Regulation 2

13

Abortion

The termination of a pregnancy has been a criminal offence for a long time. The effect of the Abortion Act 1967 was to legalize the termination of a pregnancy under certain circumstances which are set out below.

Legal grounds for a termination of pregnancy

The termination of a pregnancy will be lawful if two medical practitioners, in good faith, are of the opinion that one of four grounds apply. The grounds may be summarized as follows[1]:

1. The pregnancy has not passed the end of the 24th week and its continuance would involve a greater risk to the physical or mental health of the pregnant woman or any existing children of her family than the risk to her (or to the children's) physical or mental health if the pregnancy is terminated.
2. The termination is necessary to prevent grave permanent injury to the physical or mental health of the pregnant woman.
3. The continuance of the pregnancy would involve a greater risk to the life of the pregnant woman than the risk to her life if the pregnancy is terminated.
4. There is a substantial risk that if the child were born it would suffer from such physical or mental abnormalities as to be seriously handicapped.

Selective removal of any fetus in a multiple pregnancy is also lawful if one of grounds 1, 2 or 3 are met. If ground 4 is used then the termination must be of the fetus that has been identified as having a substantial risk of being seriously handicapped.

The strict 24 week time limit applies only to the first ground and so it can be seen that a pregnancy could be terminated after that time if, say, a child was going to be born seriously handicapped. It is important to note that the risk of the child being born seriously handicapped must be 'substantial'. The absence of a time limit could create ethical and legal problems if the pregnancy was relatively advanced and there is no definition of what amounts to 'seriously handicapped'. Legal advice would be recommended before proceeding if the fetus was capable of being born alive.

In determining any risk to the woman's physical or mental health in grounds 1 and 2 above, account must be taken of the actual or reasonably foreseeable environment of the woman. In urgent situations the opinion of only one doctor is required if the termination is immediately necessary to save life or prevent a grave permanent injury to the woman's physical or mental health[2].

The termination must take place in an NHS hospital or in a facility approved by the Secretary of State for Health (unless it is an urgent situation as set out above), and must be under the overall responsibility of a doctor. The doctor must prescribe the treatment and remain responsible for it, but the treatment may be actually carried out by other staff as long as it is in accordance with the doctor's directions[3].

For example, a doctor was charged with having performed an illegal abortion. A pregnant woman was referred by her GP to a gynaecologist for a termination of pregnancy. The woman said that no internal examination was performed and no questions were asked about her medical history but she was asked why she wanted an abortion. She said that she was not in love and was frightened by the idea of childbirth.

A short time later the woman was admitted for the termination. The woman said that she did not see another doctor before the procedure. The anaesthetist, however, said that he gave the required second opinion and then administered the anaesthetic. The certificate A had been signed by both doctors, although it had been alleged that this was a forgery but this accusation was rejected by the jury.

At the trial the gynaecologist's defence was that, first, he had formed the opinion required for the Abortion Act in good faith and, secondly, when he came to do the termination the woman was in the process of having a miscarriage. The jury convicted him of the charges and this was upheld by the Court of Appeal[4].

Conscientious objection

Abortion is a subject about which people have very strong feelings. There is provision in section 4 of the Act for those with a conscientious objection to be excluded from any obligation to participate in any abortion taking place under the Act. This exemption is limited to those people actually taking part in the treatment. For example, a doctor's secretary was not covered by the exemption when she refused to type a letter referring a patient for an abortion. Her dismissal for misconduct was upheld[5]. However, if it is an emergency required to save life or prevent grave permanent injury to the woman's physical or mental health, then the conscientious objection exemption does not apply.

Requirements to comply with the Act

For termination of pregnancy the following conditions must be fulfilled[6].

1 (a) In the non-urgent situation: Two doctors must, in good faith, have come to one of the opinions 1–4 set out above and have completed a form known as 'certificate A' before the termination of pregnancy starts.

(b) In the urgent situation (as described above): The single doctor's opinion must be recorded on 'certificate B' either before treatment or, if that is not reasonably practical, as soon as possible but not later than 24 hours after the treatment.

2 After the termination a completed formal notice must be sent to the Chief Medical Officer in a sealed envelope within 7 days. There are restrictions on disclosure of the notice or any information given to the Chief Medical Officer. Disclosure is permitted to, amongst others, a doctor with the woman's written consent and to the GMC. It is also permitted for the purposes of bona fide research, or for the police to investigate a crime under the Act.

Does the father have any rights?

The short answer to that question is 'no'. It is not possible for a father, whether he is married to the pregnant woman or not, to prevent a lawful abortion under the Abortion Act as he has no rights under the Act. It might be possible to stop an abortion if it was not lawful, but that would not be dependent on the relationship between the mother and father but on the criminal nature of the abortion[7].

Summary

A termination of pregnancy will be lawful if one of the four grounds set out in the Abortion Act 1967 is met. Abortions outside the scope of the Act are criminal offences.

References

1 Abortion Act 1967, section 1(1)
2 Abortion Act 1967, section 1(4)
3 Royal College of Nursing (UK) v DHSS [1981] 1 All ER 545
4 R v Smith (John) [1973] 1 WLR 1510
5 Janaway v Salford Health Authority [1988] 3 All ER 1079
6 The Abortion Regulations 1991, SI 1991 No. 499
7 Paton v Trustees of BPAS and another [1978] 2 All ER 987 and C v S [1987] 1 All ER 1241

14

Wills, powers of attorney and the Court of Protection

Patients may want to make a will whilst they are in hospital and make arrangements for their finances to be dealt with in the event that they should become unable to manage their affairs. Any such patient should obtain their own legal advice but health care staff can get involved when they are asked to give opinions about a patient's mental capacity or to sign or witness various documents.

Wills

A will is the way a person (who is generally over eighteen years of age) can dispose of his or her property after their death. The person making the will is called a testator if male and a testatrix if female. The will appoints executors to carry out the testator's wishes. If a person dies without making a will the law makes provision for the distribution of the estate and the people given the task of the distribution are called administrators. Executors and administrators are given the collective title of personal representatives.

For a will to be valid there are various legal requirements which must be met. A vital requirement is that a person must have the necessary mental capacity to make a will. Doctors may become involved if there is any doubt over the testator's capacity. A person has 'testamentary capacity' if[1]:

1. He or she understands what a will is, its effect and what may affect its operation.
2. He or she understands what property there is to be disposed of. It is unlikely that the precise values or every item have to be known, but there must be a realization of the size of the estate.
3. He or she understands who the people are who ought to expect to benefit from the estate.

A doctor may be asked by a patient's solicitor to assess the patient's mental capacity to make a will. The purpose is to help determine whether testamentary capacity exists and to be able to prove it later in the event of a challenge to the will on that basis. In general, a testator must have capacity when he gives the solicitor instructions to draw up the will *and* when he signs it. Therefore, if capacity is assessed by a doctor it is likely that the solicitor will wish the doctor to witness the will as well as to demonstrate capacity at that time. The doctor should make records of his findings and conclusions on both occasions to which reference can be made at a later date if necessary.

Some hospitals have policies which state that hospital clinical staff should not witness wills. There is no legal reason why they should not, but if they do it is possible that they could become involved in a dispute between members of the patient's family after his or her death over whether there really was capacity to make a will. The fact of witnessing the will may be taken to indicate an assessment of the patient's capacity even though no formal assessment has taken place. If a doctor is asked to witness a will it is advisable to determine whether testamentary capacity is in doubt.

It would be far better for it to be made clear by the patient's solicitor that an assessment of capacity was required, which could then be arranged. Alternatively, if witnesses are needed non-health care staff could be asked, or people from outside the hospital brought in, to carry out the task.

Before carrying out any assessment it is worthwhile considering the following:

1. Is the doctor competent to undertake the assessment?
2. Has the solicitor given written instructions so that the doctor knows what the current legal test for capacity is and is aware of other information necessary to make the assessment? For example, the doctor needs to know the extent of the patient's property (whether the patient remembers his property cannot be assessed when the doctor does not know the true extent of it).
3. Have any problems of confidentiality been overcome?
4. Does the doctor have indemnity cover? This would not be covered under the NHS indemnity and there could be a claim for a negligently performed assessment.

It is important to realize that a person who has a mental illness, or who has been given any diagnostic label, may be able to make a valid will. In each case the test of capacity remains the same and it is a matter of fact as to whether the capacity exists. For guidance on how to assess capacity in this and other situations see *Assessment of Mental Capacity—Guidance for Doctors and Lawyers* produced by the Law Society and the BMA[2].

The patient's solicitor should inform any witness to a will of the necessary requirements. The following conditions need to be fulfilled[3]:

1. A witness must *not* be a beneficiary of the will or a spouse of a beneficiary, otherwise the gift is void.
2. A witness must watch the testator sign the will and remain until he or she has finished and there must be at least one other witness present at the same time.
3. A witness must sign the will in the presence of the testator.

Powers of attorney

A power of attorney is a formal document where somebody (the donor) gives another person (the attorney) the power to deal with their financial affairs and property (with some specific exceptions).

Ordinary power of attorney and enduring power of attorney

The significant difference between these two types of power of attorney is that an ordinary one is automatically revoked if the donor becomes mentally incapable. However, an enduring power of attorney[4] survives if the donor becomes incapable, by reason of mental disorder, of managing and administering his property and affairs. The two types of power of attorney are designed for different purposes. The ordinary power is for those who need another person to act for them for a temporary period whilst the donor cannot act in person. On the other hand, the enduring power of attorney is beneficial if it is expected or possible that the donor will lose his or her capacity to manage their affairs. The donor can decide how much responsibility to give the attorney by altering the terms of the document. Once the power of attorney documents have been signed they are effective and the attorney can act as well as the donor. If the donor loses his mental capacity the attorney alone has power to act under an enduring power of attorney until it is revoked or replaced. As stated above, an ordinary power of attorney ceases to be effective if the donor loses capacity.

To have capacity to grant an enduring power of attorney the donor must understand the nature and effect of the power. There are four criteria to determine capacity:

1. The donor must understand that the attorney will be able to assume complete authority over the donor's affairs.
2. The donor must understand that the attorney will be able to do anything with the donor's property that the donor would have done.

3. The donor must understand that the authority will continue if the donor is or becomes mentally incapable.
4. The donor must understand that if he or she is or becomes mentally incapable, the power will be irrevocable without confirmation by the Court of Protection[5].

(Points 1 and 2 may not always be included in the power of attorney.)

The requirements of the test for capacity mean that a person can still grant an enduring power of attorney even if they have already lost the ability to manage their own property and affairs, as long as the four criteria above are satisfied[5].

Again, before carrying out an assessment, it is suggested that regard is given to the list set out above on assessing capacity for wills and the guidance in the Law Society and BMA book on the assessment of mental capacity[2].

The Court of Protection and an enduring power of attorney

Once an attorney has reason to believe that the donor is becoming or has become mentally incapable, he or she must give notice to the donor and various relatives of the donor. Having done that the attorney must register the enduring power of attorney with the Court of Protection[6]. The Court of Protection is part of the Supreme Court and acts in a supervisory and regulatory role in this context.

Incapacity to manage property and affairs

If a person who has not made an enduring power of attorney becomes incapable, by reason of mental disorder, of managing and administering his or her property and affairs, then that management can be carried out by a 'Receiver' if an application is made to the Court of Protection for appointment of a Receiver. The application must be accompanied by a medical certificate known as a CP3. This form has guidance notes for its completion and again reference should be made to the Law Society and BMA book[2] referred to above.

In summary, it is a prerequisite that the person is suffering from a mental disorder as defined by section 1 of the Mental Health Act 1983 (see Chapter 8). The mental disorder must be the reason why the person cannot manage their affairs. An assessment has also to be made of the patient's capacity to deal with their affairs, which will depend, amongst other things, on the complexity of those affairs.

Statutory wills

If a person whose affairs are being dealt with by the Court of Protection expresses a desire to make a will, the matter should be referred to the court. If the person lacks testamentary capacity as well, then the Court of Protection can prepare a statutory will. However, if there is testamentary capacity then a will can be prepared under the court's supervision.

Summary

There are a variety of ways for a person to ensure that their financial affairs are dealt with should they be unable to do so. Medical staff may become involved because of the need to establish the mental capacity of the person giving up control of their affairs.

References

1 Banks v Goodfellow (1870) LR 5 QB 549
2 British Medical Association and Law Society (1995) *Assessment of Mental Capacity—Guidance for Doctors and Lawyers*
3 Wills Act 1837, sections 9 and 15
4 Enduring Power of Attorney Act 1985, section 1
5 Re K, Re F [1988] All ER 358
6 Enduring Power of Attorney Act 1985, section 4

15

Post mortems and transplantation

The question of who owns a body and parts of a body can be a difficult legal issue. The law regulates the performance of post mortems and the removal of body parts for treatment, research and education without having to address the question of ownership of the body and its parts. Instead, the law is based on the wishes of the patient/donor and/or the agreement of the next of kin if the patient has died. The relevant statutes are the Human Tissue Act 1961 (HTA) and the Human Organ Transplants Act 1989 (HOTA).

Post mortems

A coroner has the power to obtain a post mortem to establish the cause of death and to further his inquiry into a death (see Chapter 10). Nothing must be done to interfere with the coroner's investigation and if there is reason to believe that a coroner's post mortem or inquiry may be required then the matter *must* be referred to the coroner[1]. If the treating staff wish to carry out a post mortem, the reasons have to be related to further understanding the cause of death for research and/or education. If the cause of death is unknown, the case should be referred to the coroner (or if it comes within any other categories where the coroner should be involved). On the basis that it is not a coroner's case, a post mortem will be lawful if[3]:

1. It is carried out by a fully registered medical practitioner or according to his or her instructions.
2. There is no reason to believe that the deceased had objected to a post mortem and had not changed his/her mind.
3. There is no reason to believe that the surviving spouse and any surviving relatives object to the post mortem.

In order to ascertain points 2 and 3 such reasonable inquiry as is practicable must be made. It is likely that asking the husband/wife or other relatives present at the hospital (or with whom contact has been made during the patient's illness) whether they are aware of any objections is sufficient. Although it is not a legal requirement, a form is usually signed to record the lack of objection. This is a matter of evidence in the event of any later problems.

If the above criteria are met then 'the person in lawful possession of the body' may authorize the post mortem. This phrase is not defined and it may be difficult to determine what it means if a patient has died in a hospital or nursing home. Some decided cases indicate that the person in lawful possession is the hospital authority and some that it is the executors/next of kin. In practical terms, it should not cause a problem because if there are any relatives who object, then the person in lawful possession cannot authorize the post mortem anyway. However, if a person dies without any next of kin/spouse then the relevant hospital manager can give the lawful authority for a post mortem. Importantly, an undertaker or other similar person who has the body for internment or cremation is specifically prevented from authorizing a post mortem[2].

Removal of body parts

The legal criteria that have to be met depend on whether the purpose for the removal of tissue is transplantation and on whether the donor is alive or dead.

Prohibition on buying or selling organs

It is unlawful to deal in organs for transplantation. This includes offering to sell an organ or looking to buy one. This prohibition applies whether the organ is from a living or dead donor. It is also an offence to advertise organs for sale or to invite people to sell their organs[4].

Removal from a living donor

If the tissue to be removed is for education, research, diagnostic or therapeutic purposes other than transplantation then all that is required is the appropriate consent of the donor/patient.

If the organ is for transplantation then, for the removal of the organ and its transplantation to be lawful, the following must apply[5]: (1) the donor and recipient must be genetically related; or (2) if the transplantation is between unrelated individuals, the Unrelated Live Transplant Regulatory Authority (ULTRA) must authorize the procedure[7].

Where donor and recipient are genetically related

The types of relatives are restricted so that the transplant is lawful only if the relation is one of the following:

- Natural parents and children.
- Brothers and sisters of whole or half blood.
- Brothers and sisters of whole or half blood of either of the patient's natural parents.
- The natural children of the patient's brothers and sisters of whole or half blood or of the brothers or sisters of whole or half blood of either of the patient's natural parents.

The relationship must be determined by genetic tests based on DNA variations. The tests must be carried out and interpreted by an approved person and he/she must state, in writing, that the necessary genetic relationship exists. The tester also specifies the tests and who it is necessary to test in addition to the donor and recipient[6].

Transplantation between unrelated individuals

Transplantation between unrelated individuals will only be lawful if the Unrelated Live Transplant Regulatory Authority (ULTRA) has authorized the procedure[7]. In order to give an authorization ULTRA must be satisfied on several grounds. These are as follows:

1. No payment has been made or will be made (i.e. prohibition on commercial dealing in section 1 of HOTA).
2. The doctor who has referred the case to ULTRA has clinical responsibility for the donor.
3. Various further conditions are satisfied (unless the removal of the donor's organ is for the donor's treatment), which are:
   (a) the doctor has given the donor an explanation of the nature of the medical procedure for the organ removal and the risks involved;
   (b) the donor understands the information in (a) and consents;
   (c) the donor's consent was freely given (no duress, coercion or offer of an inducement);
   (d) the donor understands that he/she is entitled to withdraw consent if he/she wishes but has not done so;
   (e) the donor and recipient have both been interviewed by a person who appears to ULTRA to have been suitably qualified to conduct such interviews and who has reported to ULTRA on the conditions set out in (a)–(d) above and has included in their report an account of any difficulties of communication with the donor or the recipient and an explanation of how those difficulties were overcome.

Removal from a dead body

The use of a body or body parts from a dead person for the purposes of medical education, research or therapy may be authorized by the 'person lawfully in possession of the body' if certain criteria are met[8]. These are as follows:

1. The deceased has expressed, in writing at any time, a request that his/her body or any specified part of the body was to be used for the purposes set out above.
2. If, instead of in writing, the deceased during his last illness, in the presence of two witnesses, orally made the request in point 1 above.
3. The person in lawful possession of the body has no reason to believe that the request in points 1 or 2 was not subsequently withdrawn (whether orally or in writing).

As discussed above, the meaning of the phrase 'the person lawfully in possession of the body' is unclear. Given the ambiguity, breaching the law can be avoided by obtaining the authorization from the hospital authority and the deceased's next of kin. Furthermore, this may be the ethically appropriate step. If the deceased's request was oral then the two witnesses should record the details of the request and the date, time and place that it was made. This is as evidence in case of any later problems.

The removal of any parts from a dead body may be authorized by the person lawfully in possession of the body for therapeutic purposes or for purposes of medical education or research[9]. This is even in the absence of a request from the deceased if, having made such reasonable enquiry as may be practicable, he has *no* reason to believe either of the following:

1. That the deceased had expressed an objection to his body being dealt with in that way after death and had not withdrawn it.
2. That the surviving spouse or any surviving relative of the deceased objects to the body being dealt with in that way.

As under post mortems above, it is likely that asking the next of kin who have visited the hospital would represent sufficient enquiry to cover the issues above. A written record should be made for use as evidence if necessary at a later date.

The removal of body parts must be carried out by a registered medical practitioner unless the part to be removed is an eye or part of an eye[10]. In that case it can be done on the instruction of a registered medical practitioner who is satisfied that the person who is to do the removal is sufficiently qualified and trained to perform the operation competently. Before any removal takes place the registered medical practitioner must personally examine the body and be satisfied that the person is dead.

If the removal of an eye or part of an eye is not to be carried out personally by a doctor, then the doctor giving the instructions must either satisfy him or herself that the person is dead or be satisfied on the basis of a statement from another doctor who has personally examined the body. As with a post mortem, a coroner's inquiry must not be interfered with and the matter must be referred to the coroner before any steps are taken if necessary. Once again, in any of the situations given above, a person who has the body only for the purpose of its internment or cremation is not permitted to give any of the necessary authorizations.

The Anatomy Act 1984

This Act specifically controls the dissection of a dead body or body part for the purposes of teaching or studying or researching into morphology. It has a system of licensing to regulate the anatomical examination and covers the retention of specimens and disposal of the body or body parts. It is obviously of relevance to medical schools and research institutions. Bodies for dissection can be obtained either if the deceased made a request or by asking the next of kin. The precise requirements are similar to those set out above for the removal of body parts from a dead person.

Summary

The law controls the removal of body parts for various purposes including transplantation. The regulations are more rigorous for transplantation between a live donor and recipient than when an organ is taken from a person who has died.

References

1 Human Tissue Act 1961, section 1(5)
2 Human Tissue Act 1961, section 1(6)
3 Human tissue Act 1961, section 2
4 Human Organ Transplants Act 1989, section 1
5 Human Organ Transplants Act 1989, section 2
6 Human Organ Transplants (Establishment of Relationship) Regulations 1998, SI 1998 No. 1428
7 Human Organ Transplants (Unrelated Person) Regulations 1989, SI 1989 No. 2480
8 Human Tissue Act 1961, section 1
9 Human Tissue Act 1961, section 1(2)
10 Human Tissue Act 1961, sections 1(4) and 1(4A)

16

Risk management

Every organization providing a service should take steps to ensure that the standard or quality of service is maintained at the required level. Leaving this to chance is likely to mean that quality will be variable. The Government believes that the quality of care delivered by the NHS is variable and has stated its aim to provide consistently high quality health care.

Department of Health guidance[1] on quality states:

'This aim [high quality health care for all patients] will be achieved in three complementary ways, by establishing:

- Arrangements for setting clear national quality standards, through National Service Frameworks and the National Institute for Clinical Excellence.
- Mechanisms for ensuring local delivery of high quality clinical services, through clinical governance reinforced by a new statutory duty of quality and supported by programmes of lifelong learning and local delivery of professional self-regulation; and
- Effective systems for monitoring delivery of quality standards, in the form of a new statutory Commission for Health Improvement and an NHS Performance Assessment Framework, together with the first national survey of patient and user experience.

Clinical governance is a key part of a concerted 10 year programme of work throughout the NHS to improve the quality of patient care.

NHS organisations, and individuals working within them, need to monitor and improve quality in a number of ways. They must have:

- Clear lines of responsibility and accountability for the overall quality of clinical care;
- A comprehensive programme of quality improvement activities;
- Clear policies aimed at managing risk; and
- Procedures for all professional groups to identify and remedy poor performance.'

The method devised to deliver high quality health care has three elements: first, to develop and set required standards; secondly, to 'govern' the delivery of clinical care; and thirdly, to monitor performance[1]. Risk management has been incorporated as part of the second element, i.e. clinical governance.

Clinical risk management

In response to the increase in clinical negligence litigation a more formalized method of trying to deal with the problem has been introduced. The principles are common sense but the use of a structured approach is intended to improve outcomes. Risk management has been advocated by insurance companies for a long time.

Risk has been described as having two basic parts: first, the element of uncertainty or chance and secondly, the outcome[2]. Usually, the risk of something occurring refers to a negative outcome which results in a loss whether that be financial, emotional or physical. Everyday activities involve risks to which, to some extent, risk management is applied. For example, riding a bicycle at night has an increased chance of the rider being knocked off because he cannot be seen clearly by other road users. To avoid this riders have lights on their bikes and wear reflective clothing. In some areas the state imposes risk management on individuals, such as the compulsory wearing of seat belts in motor cars. The strategies are all aimed at reducing the element of chance or uncertainty.

The process

The process of risk management is broken down into three stages:

1. Identify the risk.
2. Analyse the risk.
3. Control the risk.

The process is similar to that of audit, namely, identify a standard, check performance against the standard and then modify performance to meet the standard. They are both ongoing processes that aim to improve and maintain the quality of health care.

Identification and analysis

Identification of a risk involves looking at bad outcomes and near misses in order to establish what went wrong or seeking to identify where an adverse outcome might occur in the future. Analysis of these identified areas looks at the process of how the adverse outcome might occur and the effect of the outcome in personal and financial terms, as well as the likely frequency of occurrence. There is a lot to be gained simply by observing and talking to those involved in the process of identifying and analysing risks. There are, however, commercial organizations who can be employed to carry out risk assessments, often using complicated techniques of risk identification and analysis.

Control

There are some risks that can never be eliminated or avoided and these can only be reduced. Even in the most skilful hands, there will always be the risk of a complication during an operation because there are factors which occur outside the sphere of control. Some risks have to be accepted.

Furthermore, there may be some risks that occur with great frequency but have little or no effect, and others that occur rarely but with very significant effect. Some form of assessment of whether it is feasible or worthwhile to control an identified risk needs to be undertaken. The question of the availability of resources will also feature in this analysis. There would be little point in devoting money and human resources to deal with a risk that had little or no effect whilst other, more significant, risks existed. Priorities have to be set because it is impossible to deal with all identified risks.

Control of risk can be broken down into two areas, which might be termed accident prevention and damage limitation.

Accident prevention

The main aim of risk management is the prevention and minimization of risk, i.e. avoiding adverse outcomes. This primary prevention may be achieved by continuing education, supervision and adequate training. Audit is also a method of preventing adverse outcomes by checking that practice is reaching the expected standard.

One of the most common methods of controlling risks is the use of guidelines/protocols. These allow for each step in a treatment process to be identified and followed, and they reduce the risk of one of those steps being omitted by a less experienced practitioner or by simple human error. Some of the disadvantages are that they can be inflexible and there may be problems in dealing with a legal claim if the treatment given deviates from the protocol/guidelines, as the protocol itself may be seen as evidence of the standard that the clinician was expected to reach. If a protocol is not followed then the reasons for this need to be clear and supported by a responsible body of medical opinion to avoid a finding of negligence (see Chapter 3). Another problem with protocols is that they become outdated. They must be dated and old copies kept so that, in the event of a claim, the appropriate protocol may be consulted.

Some people are concerned about whether a document should be entitled 'protocol' or 'guideline' as the former gives the impression that it *must* be followed and the latter that it is less prescriptive. It would be preferable to use the term 'guideline' if that is what the document is intended to be and reserve 'protocol' for those cases where there is more of an element of compulsion. However, in each case it would depend on all the facts and the intention behind the document. In other words, if a document headed 'guideline' were written in such a way that it *must* be followed then having termed it a guideline will not help.

Damage limitation

Risk management is also important after an event, as steps can be taken to minimize the adverse outcome. This is usually the area that most interests lawyers, as they deal predominantly with cases once the damage has occurred. Some important aspects of this area are detailed below.

Record keeping

For many years health care workers have been asked to make comprehensive notes by the organizations that indemnify them in the event of a claim. The reason for this is that, by the time a claim has arisen, several years may have passed. The health care staff involved, even if they can all be located, probably do not recall the event and thus have to rely on the records. Furthermore, if a witness can recall an event then contemporaneous records help to support that recollection.

The patient is unlikely to have records but, in all probability, it will be the only time that such an event has occurred to him/her, which is a good reason for it to have lodged in his/her memory. If there is a conflict between what the patient and the clinician say happened, then it is more likely to be decided in favour of the patient in the absence of a specific recollection or support from a note.

After the event witness comments

Although notes written before the event are the best type of record it is useful to make notes after the event to fill in any gaps. If such notes are made in the medical records it is vital to ensure that the existing notes are not altered. Any such alterations will be treated with extreme suspicion later. The subsequent entry should be correctly dated and an explanation given to identify why it has been written later.

Statements or comments from witnesses may be obtained as part of an incident investigation. It is best to keep to a factual narrative which fills in any relevant gaps in the story and includes the reasons for decisions. Commentary on the actions of others is best avoided apart from describing what else was going on when working in a team. Straight regurgitation of the medical records is not helpful, apart from explaining abbreviations or poor handwriting. Giving opinions can cause difficulties, as they may be given without the full facts or even the necessary expertise. If anyone feels that their conduct could be called into question they should seek advice before committing anything to paper, as any documentation may not be confidential (even if it states that it is) in the event of a legal claim. This is unlike the situation in which the statement is being taken predominantly for a legal claim, when it will be confidential. For those claims covered by the NHS indemnity it would be appropriate to discuss the case with the Trust's legal manager as the Trust will be the defendant in any proceedings. Otherwise, independent advice should be taken.

Incident reporting
The reporting of adverse incidents and near misses is considered to be a key part of any risk management programme. It provides information about events that allow identification and analysis of risks. Incident reporting triggers a damage limitation investigation.

Summary

It is best to think of risk management as a positive force to maintain and improve the quality of patient care. Other significant benefits that then follow are the minimization of exposure to legal claims and improved chances of defending claims once an adverse incident has occurred.

References

1 Department of Health/NHS Executive (1999) *Clinical Governance: Quality in the New NHS*. HSC 1999/065
2 Dickson, G.C.A. (1991) *Risk and Insurance*. Chartered Insurance Institute

17

Defending a clinical negligence claim

A claim starts with an adverse outcome which is either real or perceived as such by the patient. It may be some time after the event, possibly years, when the patient realizes that they may have a potential claim and this may occur after they have received medical or legal advice.

Limitation on bringing claims

There is a time limit which prevents claims from being brought after a certain period of time has elapsed since the event in question. In clinical negligence cases this limit is three years but it may be extended under certain circumstances. The time limit runs from the date of the negligence (and the breach of contractual duty in the case of a private patient) or from the date that the injured person has knowledge of certain factors which make up the claim (these are set out in the Limitation Act 1980[1]). The knowledge can be actual, in the sense that the person is aware that something went wrong, or 'constructive'. Constructive knowledge means that the person is 'deemed to know' on the basis that they would reasonably be expected to acquire the knowledge from observable or ascertainable facts including obtaining medical or other expert help[2]. For example, a court deemed that a patient who attended to have an operation to save his leg had constructive knowledge of the potential negligence because, after the operation, he had lost his leg. This outcome was the reverse of the intended one and should have made the patient enquire into the circumstances[3].

Under certain circumstances the three year time limit is altered. Children have three years from their eighteenth birthday in which to bring a claim that arose during their minority. Those people who are incapable, by reason of mental disorder (as defined in the Mental Health Act 1983), of managing and administering their own property and affairs (technically referred to as 'patients') have no time limit whilst they remain under a disability. If they regain capacity, the three year limit runs from that date.

Furthermore, the court has a discretion to allow a claim to proceed even if the time limit has expired[4]. In exercising this power there are various factors to be considered, including balancing the prejudice that the parties might suffer by making or not making a decision to allow the claim to proceed and the length of the delay and reasons for it.

Consequences of the time limits

Bringing a claim may be difficult if the time limit since the incident has passed, as it can be difficult to overcome the 'date of knowledge' test discussed above. Not all cases are as obvious as having lost a leg that was meant to be saved, and patients may not realize that they have a claim until they receive expert evidence or legal advice. Claims *are* brought and proceed after the initial three year period has elapsed and the consequence for a defendant is that they cannot be absolutely certain that a claim will not arise several years after the event. In the case of incidents involving under-eighteen year olds or 'patients' (as defined above) the time for bringing a claim is considerably longer. This means that a defendant may have to deal with allegations going back many years. This is one of the reasons why accurate and comprehensive records are important and why records should be kept safely. Records should be kept for longer than the time limit for claims because of this risk. However, the more time that has passed since the incident, the lower the risk of a claim materializing. For example, the NHS guidelines recommend that records for adults should be kept for a minimum of eight years after the last treatment episode, obstetric records for twenty-five years, children's records until their twenty-fifth birthday or twenty-sixth if treatment ended when they were seventeen, and for patients suffering from mental health problems the records should be kept for twenty years from the date when no more treatment was considered necessary. If the patient dies it is recommended that the notes are kept for eight years from the date of death (in obstetric records the retention should be governed by the death of the child)[5]. To make the risk as low as possible it would be ideal to keep all original records for ever but this is not practical and a cut-off point has to be reached by the holder of any records.

One of the obvious problems with the length of time that may elapse before a claim is fading of witnesses' memories of the events. This is the reason why part of a risk management strategy involves collecting statements after an adverse incident. In addition, clinicians may not identify potential claims and a risk management programme should aim to pick them up.

Pre-Action Protocol

A protocol, called the 'Pre-Action Protocol'[6], for the resolution of clinical disputes before proceedings has been devised by the Clinical Disputes Forum (CDF). The CDF was formed following Lord Woolf's inquiry[7] into civil litigation and has members from various parties interested in clinical negligence including representatives of doctors' interests and lawyers who act for patients and defendants.

The aims of the protocol include increasing the openness when something 'goes wrong' and decreasing the mistrust between the parties in clinical disputes so that deserving cases are settled and other non-deserving cases do not proceed. In essence, the protocol encourages parties to give full information and to set out their case in accordance with a timetable. For example, disclosure of relevant records should occur within 40 days and any delay communicated to the party making the request. The protocol has the support of the NHS Executive, the medical defence organizations and the General Medical Council. It has been incorporated into the Civil Procedure Rules which govern the conduct of clinical negligence cases, and parties who have not followed the protocol may be penalized once the litigation has commenced. Compliance with the protocol is therefore an essential part of the clinical negligence process.

Request for records

One of the first indications of a claim is often a request for the medical records by the patient and their solicitors. Patients have a right of access to their medical records anyway[8] but where the patient and holder of the records are likely to be parties to a claim the right to disclosure of documentation before any legal proceedings have started is wider than just the medical notes. Documents which adversely affect or support either party's case can be obtained; for example, any documents that were made after an investigation or complaint, including the personal notes of people involved in the case[9]. This is the case even if they are marked 'private and confidential' or with other similar terms, all of which have no effect. The only documents that are not disclosable are those which have been created for the predominant purpose of litigation and are therefore covered by 'legal privilege'. For example, if a legal claim was thought to be likely and statements were taken because of that possibility, then legal privilege is likely to apply. However, if those statements were obtained for the investigation of a complaint, then they will be disclosable. Most experienced solicitors send letters that are widely drafted, requesting different types of documents including complaints correspondence.

More formal stage of a claim

After disclosure of the records and any other documents there will be a period when nothing is heard from the claimant. This is because, in order to identify whether he or she has a case, medical experts' reports will have to be obtained. This can take several months. Having obtained the reports, the lawyers will consider and advise on whether or not to proceed and whether any further evidence is required. There may be a temptation on the part of the defendant to ignore the warning signs and believe that a claim will not proceed. This is no longer a wise course of action as the next stage of the litigation process has to be dealt with in a relatively short time.

When the claimant has completed his or her investigations the next stage is to send a 'letter of claim'. This letter should set out:

1. The facts of the case.
2. What the allegations of negligence are.
3. The injury suffered, including the condition and progress.
4. Any claim for financial losses (if possible).

Relevant documents should be referred to and copies provided if the defendant does not have them. This letter starts a timetable and the defendant has three months to send a letter of response. In practical terms, as said above, this is a very short time to respond unless the case is straightforward, as statements will be needed from the witnesses and possibly also an expert report.

If the claimant is short of time because the limitation period is about to expire, then he/she may have to issue court proceedings anyway to avoid this problem. In these circumstances, the court is likely to allow the defendant time to investigate the case.

The response to the letter of claim must answer the allegations and should do more that just deny any negligence. If any areas are identified where there has been a failure to meet the required standard, then these may be admitted. The aim of the letter of claim and response is to give the parties better information at an early stage and to promote the resolution of claims.

Starting the court process

If the claim has not been resolved then it is open to the injured party to start formal court proceedings. The party making the claim is known as the 'claimant' (formerly the plaintiff) and the party defending as the 'defendant'. The claimant has to prepare formal documentation which includes the claim form and the accompanying 'particulars of claim'. The particulars of claim is the name for the document in which the claimant sets out his or her version of events and the matters that he or she alleges constitute the negligence. This will be based on the supportive medical expert's report. These documents are then sent to the court and issued and served on the defendant (for the identity of the defendant, see Chapter 2), together with a medical report and a schedule of the financial loss that is claimed.

Service of proceedings (i.e. the claim form etc.) starts another timetable. The defendant has a maximum of 28 days, or 56 days if the claimant agrees, to serve a defence. If the defendant cannot comply with the timetable, the court can be asked to allow more time.

The defence must respond to the particulars of claim and, again, a straight denial is not enough. If a defence is not served, the claimant is entitled to obtain judgement automatically.

Both the particulars of claim and the defence have to be verified by a 'statement of truth'. This means that the party signing the document has an honest belief that its contents are true. It is a criminal offence to make, or cause to be made, a statement of truth without such an honest belief.

Management of the case

Once the defence has been served, the court will decide on how quickly the case will come to trial and make 'directions' which set out a timetable for the steps to be taken before any trial. The underlying motives of the directions are to let each party see what the other party's evidence is before trial and to narrow the issues. This involves:

- Providing copies of relevant documents (disclosure).
- Exchanging lay and expert evidence in the form of statements and reports respectively.
- Having a meeting of experts to see on which areas they agree.

Documents

Documents mean any items in which information is recorded and the term includes radiographs, scans and electronically stored information as well as paper records. The parties have to prepare a list documenting those items on which they rely and those which do not support their case, as well as those which help or do not support their opponent's case. The list has to be verified personally by the party (i.e. not their lawyers) to state that a reasonable search for documents has been undertaken. Such documents will include notes made by clinicians after the event or complaints correspondence as discussed above.

Witness statements

Witness statements stand as the main piece of evidence of a witness at a trial and therefore it is vital that they are complete (although the witness is able to amplify their evidence at trial). They are one of the major pieces of evidence on which the experts will base their opinions.

In addition to certain requirements for layout, witness statements must:

1. Include the full name and address of the witness and his occupation and position held, plus the name and address of the employer.
2. Be expressed in the first person and state which parts are repeated from memory and which statements are from records or from knowledge of usual practice.
3. Provide certain details of the witness's experience and qualifications.
4. Be verified by a statement of truth (see above).

It is unlikely that a witness will have perfect first-hand recall of events. However, statements of what must have happened because of entries in the notes or based on usual practice are also valid evidence. In some cases it may be the only evidence available. It is important to consider that the judge is unlikely to have any relevant medical expertise and technical terminology will need to be explained. Furthermore, a technical term or shorthand note can encompass a large amount of information and this needs to be spelt out in detail. For example, 'chest NAD' means 'I did not detect any abnormalities when I examined the chest'. Details of the chest examination may need to be spelt out; for example: 'I visually inspected the patient's chest. His respiratory rate was not elevated and both sides moved equally with normal expansion.' This would be important if, say, the allegations were that a lobar pneumonia had been missed on examination. The experts and court will want to know that a proper (supported by a responsible body of medical opinion) examination of the chest took place.

Expert evidence

The next chapter deals with details concerning experts and their evidence.

The 'conference with counsel'

It is usual for there to be a meeting between the defendant's factual and expert witnesses at some stage in a case, although it may not occur if the issues are clear. The meeting is generally led by the lawyer, usually a barrister (also referred to as 'counsel'), who is to present the case to the court in the event of a trial. The conference (known as a consultation if it is with Queen's Counsel) gives the legal team an opportunity to test the evidence of the factual and expert witnesses and, as a result, to give further advice to their client. This is a vital process when planning how to deal with a case and many features that might not otherwise have been discovered until trial can emerge.

The trial

The vast majority of cases do not come to trial. The claimant may decide that they do not have a case or it may be that it has to be settled because there is no defence. In between these two extremes lie the risks of litigation. There may be different factual accounts, absent witnesses, poor records and poor recollection, to name but a few of the factors to take into account when deciding on the chances of winning or losing at trial. Furthermore, litigation is very expensive and the size of any damages and the risks involved may not make it worthwhile to proceed. A case may be settled at any stage of the litigation process before a judgement is given, including pre-proceedings.

A clinical negligence trial will take place without a jury. The judge decides the facts and makes a decision based upon the law. The witnesses and experts may sit in court until they have to give evidence. It is usual for the claimant's legal representatives to be on the left-hand side and the defendant's on the right. The side on whose behalf a witness has been called to give evidence should look after the witness and let him or her know what they have to do and what is happening.

When the judge enters the court all those present must stand and bow. The claimant's advocate (usually a barrister) outlines the case and then calls evidence. The usual order is the claimant's factual witnesses followed by the defendant's. The claimant's experts are then followed by the defendant's. This order of witnesses may be altered according to the nature of the case.

On being called, the witness either takes an oath or affirms that they will tell the truth and then gives their evidence (known as 'evidence in chief'). This may now be in the form of the witness statement previously exchanged with the other party. If not, the advocate of the party who has asked the witness to give evidence asks questions to bring out the relevant information. The advocate for the other party is then able to cross-examine the witness to test the evidence and elucidate details in an attempt to support his or her case. The witness may then be re-examined by the first advocate to deal with any points arising in cross-examination. At any stage the judge may question the witness. Throughout all of these exchanges the answers to questions should be given to the judge who, in the High Court, is addressed as 'My Lord/Lady' and 'Your Lordship/Ladyship'. In the County Court the form of address is 'Your Honour'. It is best to talk at the speed of the judge's pen, as he or she will be making a note of the evidence. If the evidence is interrupted, for example by lunch, then the witness must not talk about the case with anyone until they have finished giving evidence.

After all the evidence has been given, the advocate for the claimant will make a closing speech to summarize the evidence, the law and how it all supports his or her client's case. The defence advocate will then do the same.

It is up to the claimant to prove his or her case with the evidence produced to the court. The judge determines the facts 'on the balance of probabilities'; in other words, on a more likely than not, or greater than 50 per cent, basis. The judge does not have to be satisfied 'beyond all reasonable doubt' as in criminal cases.

The judge may give a judgement immediately or he/she may reserve judgement to a later date. In clinical negligence cases it is usual for the judgement to be reserved. The judgement identifies the findings of fact that the judge has made, the relevant law and the reasons why a particular party has won having applied the facts to the law. If the claimant has won, the judgement will also identify the award of damages.

Summary

Defending a clinical negligence claim can be a long process. It depends upon identifying the factual evidence and then obtaining expert opinion to comment on the facts. The opportunity to negotiate the settlement of a case exists from the moment a claim is first initiated to any time before judgement is given at trial. If a case is not settled then formal steps prior to trial are arranged to ensure that all parties know the evidence and case before any hearing, so that cases that can be settled are settled before a trial starts.

References

1 Limitation Act 1980, sections 11 and 14
2 Nash v Eli Lilly and Co. [1993] 4 All ER 383

3 Forbes v Wandsworth Health Authority [1996] 7 Med LR 175
4 Limitation Act 1980, section 33
5 NHS Executive (1999) *For the Record, Appendix B.* HSC 1999/053
6 Clinical Disputes Forum (1998) *Pre-Action Protocol for the Resolution of Clinical Disputes*
7 The Right Honourable Lord Woolf, Master of the Rolls (1996) *Access to Justice Final Report* HMSO
8 Access to Health Records Act 1990. (To be replaced by the Data Protection Act 1998.)
9 Civil Procedure Rules, Rule 31.16

18

Experts in civil cases

There is a big demand for expert reports from doctors and other health care professionals. This chapter deals with reports in civil proceedings (i.e. predominantly medical negligence and personal injury cases) and the requirements of the Civil Procedure Rules (CPR) part 35 which set out what use may be made of the expert evidence and the form that it must take. The general principles would be applicable to expert reports in other situations but any specific requirements should have been addressed in the letter of instruction to the expert.

Expert evidence has been subject to criticism as it has been said to increase the costs of litigation. Furthermore, experts have been criticized for becoming partisan and prolonging the litigation process rather than leading to the resolution of the issues. Part 35 of the CPR aims to deal with these problems. In some cases it is intended that there will be no oral evidence from experts. This is likely to be more common in smaller personal injury cases and, in such situations, the expert's report becomes extremely important.

Letter of instruction

The person requesting a report will send a letter of instruction to the expert. This will identify the background to the case and should explain the relevant law. It should identify what issues the expert is being asked to address and provide copies of relevant documents. Whenever a breach of duty question is being addressed (i.e. whether an act or omission fell below an acceptable standard), the expert should consider whether a breach would have made any difference to the outcome (i.e. causation). The CPR impose tight deadlines on the parties conducting litigation and the letter will probably give an indication of the time scale within which the report is required.

The issues of breach of duty and causation that are to be addressed should be answered 'on a balance of probabilities', i.e. more likely than not. This equates to anything over 50 per cent and not the statistical 95 per cent or 'beyond reasonable doubt' applicable in criminal cases which, in effect, means certainty. For example, there may have been a failure to diagnose a slipped femoral epiphysis with the subsequent development of avascular necrosis. The expert should consider the chances of avascular necrosis occurring despite earlier treatment. If this was over 50 per cent it would be more likely than not that earlier treatment would not have altered the outcome[1]. In all cases the chances of an outcome should be identified, if possible with figures. This is particularly important in condition and prognosis reports. For example, the chance of osteoarthritis in later life should be stated in cases where there has been a fracture through a joint. If there is a range of possibilities then that should be identified but an opinion given on the most likely outcome.

It may be that there are different versions of the facts. The expert's view is also important on whether the facts, as they are said to be, are possible or likely (on a balance of probabilities). For example, it may be that there are no witnesses who are able to give first-hand evidence on a particular fact (the witness may no longer be traceable or have no recollection of the event). In addition, the expert may be able to say that certain features that are claimed to have existed are not consistent with the medical condition. The expert may be able to deduce the likely answer from the evidence of the surrounding circumstances. Ultimately, the judge is the finder of fact in a case but the experts may assist the judge in determining what the facts are.

In summary, depending on the type of case, experts are going to be asked to give an opinion on all or a combination of the following: the facts as relevant to their expertise, breach of duty, causation, and condition and prognosis.

Instruction of joint experts and court appointed experts

The CPR make provision for one expert to be appointed to act for more than one of the parties in the litigation. It is likely that, before court proceedings have formally started, the parties will have tried to agree on a single expert to report. This is most likely to occur in the smaller value personal injury claims where the medical evidence is principally directed to condition and prognosis. In these circumstances, the expert will probably receive letters of instruction from each of the parties in the case. The court has the power to limit the amount of a single expert's fees and expenses and, unless otherwise stated, either of the instructing parties is responsible for all of the expert's fee.

The court also has the power to instruct an expert itself and, in this case, the expert is referred to as an assessor. The instruction may be to provide a report or attend a trial.

Who is the report for?

The rule is clear. The expert's overriding duty is to the court and not to the party that has instructed him or her. This may seem rather confusing but an expert is there to assist the court to determine the issues. The aim is to deter the manipulation of expert evidence, which may result in perpetuating an issue that, in reality, should have been eliminated. Furthermore, the expert is not giving evidence to argue the case for one side or the other. Argument is the job of the legal teams. That is not to say that the expert should ignore those who are giving the instructions. It is highly likely that the party instructing the expert will seek to clarify issues, ask for further issues to be dealt with or request amendments to reports. The expert can agree to amend as long as the opinion expressed remains that of the expert and does not conflict with his or her duty to the court.

The content of the report

The content of the report will largely be up to the expert and will depend upon the instructions that have been given. However, the CPR require certain elements to be in the report[2]. These are as outlined below:

1. The expert's qualifications.
2. Details of any literature or other material which the expert has relied on in making the report.
3. Where there is a range of opinion on the matters dealt with in the report, the expert must:
   (a) summarize the range of opinion; and
   (b) give reasons for his or her opinion.
4. A summary of conclusions reached.
5. A statement that the expert understands his duty to the court and has complied with that duty.
6. A statement setting out the substance of all material instructions (whether written or oral). The statement should summarize the facts and instructions given to the expert that are material to the opinions expressed in the report or upon which those opinions are based.
7. The report must be verified with a statement of truth as follows: 'I believe that the facts I have stated in this report are true and that the opinions I have expressed are correct.' As with any other statement

of truth, it is a criminal offence to make the statement without an honest belief in its truth.

In addition, if relevant, the report must state who carried out any test or experiment which the expert has used for the report and whether or not the test or experiment has been carried out under the expert's supervision. The qualifications of the person who carried out the test must also be stated. This is unlikely to be relevant for the majority of medical expert reports. The expert must also comply with any approved expert's protocol.

Questions to experts

Once the expert's report has been finalized, there will come a point in the proceedings when it is exchanged with the other party's (or parties') expert reports. It is usual for those reports that deal with liability issues (i.e. breach of duty and causation) to be exchanged simultaneously and those on condition and prognosis sequentially, with the claimant providing his or her report first. This process is performed by the parties' legal advisors.

After the reports have been provided, the parties have a single opportunity to put written questions to the other party's experts within 28 days[3]. The questions must be only for the purpose of clarifying the expert's report; for example, asking whether an identified failure made any difference to the outcome. The answers that the expert gives will be treated as part of the main report. The expert may well have been asked to assist in identifying any areas in the other side's expert report that should be questioned. It would be wise of the expert to make sure that the person who gave him or her instructions is aware that these questions have been served. Firstly, there may be an issue about whether the questions are appropriate (i.e. within the rules) and secondly, there may need to be discussion about the time frame for responding. The rules do not provide a time limit within which the expert has to reply but a failure to reply allows the party who asked the questions to apply to the court for an order. That order would mean that none of the expert's evidence could be used. Thirdly, there may be reasons why questions cannot be answered, and again this should be communicated as soon as possible to the person who has instructed the expert. Fourthly, it is likely that the contract between the expert and the instructing party will include a term indicating that the expert will answer such questions as are put to him or her within a reasonable time (it is important to realize that a court may say such a term is present even if it is not expressly recorded in any correspondence). It might also be negligent for an expert not to answer the question put to him under this rule. The consequences of this could be far-reaching if such a failure led to a party losing a case that they would otherwise have won. The expert might then be liable for any loss. Compliance and communication should avoid such problems but any person carrying out expert work would be well advised to have insurance.

Meetings of experts

The court wants those issues capable of resolution to be resolved before trial, and to assist with this aim the CPR include the provision to order a meeting of experts—although, of course, the parties may wish this to take place anyway. This meeting does not have to be face to face and can be over the telephone. The purpose is to identify difficult issues and/or to reach an agreement on issues if possible. The court may also specify particular issues to be discussed.

It will be important for the experts to have established exactly what it is that they have to address and the parties should have produced an agenda for the meeting to direct the experts' discussions. The discussions are protected from disclosure to the trial judge unless the parties agree otherwise and any agreement reached will not be binding on the parties without their consent. This is important, as otherwise the experts could be seen to be taking over the role of the judge and deciding the outcome of cases at the experts' meeting. Furthermore, the parties will want to make sure that any agreement between the experts has been reached on the correct legal basis, taking into account the relevant information.

At the end of a meeting the experts will be expected to produce a document setting out areas of agreement and points of disagreement with their reasons. The court may order such a statement to be made, but it is likely that the parties will want such a document anyway.

Asking the court for directions

The CPR allow an expert to make a written request for directions to help him or her carry out the duties of an expert. However, in the first instance, the expert can seek whatever information he or she needs from those instructing him or her (which may, of course, be both parties). As the expert's overriding duty is to the court, if the expert were to feel that he or she required particular details, say access to information, then the expert may write to the court setting out what it is that he or she needs. There is no requirement to tell any party of the request but the court may let a party know when it gives a direction.

Summary

The role of the medical and health care expert is vital to medical negligence and personal injury cases. The expert's overriding duty is to the court and not the instructing party. The expert's report may be the only form of evidence the court wants to see in certain cases. An expert's report must contain particular factors, which are prescribed by the Civil Procedure Rules.

References

1 Hotson v East Berkshire Health Authority [1987] 2 All ER 909
2 Civil Procedure Rules, Practice Direction 35.1.2
3 Civil Procedure Rules 35.6

Further reading

Ashton, G.R. (1995) *Elderly People and the Law*. Butterworths

British Medical Association (1995) *Advance Statements about Medical Treatment*. BMJ Publishing Group

British Medical Association (1999) *Withholding or Withdrawing Life-Prolonging Medical Treatment—Guidance for Decision Making*. BMJ Publishing Group

British Medical Association and Law Society (1995) *Assessment of Mental Capacity—Guidance for Doctors and Lawyers*

Department of Health and Welsh Office (1999) *Mental Health Act 1983 Code of Practice*. The Stationery Office

Department of Health and Welsh Office (1998) *Mental Health Act 1983 Memorandum on Parts I–VI, VIII and X*. The Stationery Office

Finch, J. (1994) *Speller's Law Relating to Hospitals*, 7th Edn. Chapman and Hall Medical

Harper, R.S. (1999) *Medical Treatment and the Law: The Protection of Adults and Minors in the Family Division*. Family Law

Jones, R.M. (1999) *Mental Health Act Manual*, 6th Edn. Sweet and Maxwell

Kennedy, I. and Grubb, A. (eds) *Medical Law Review*. Oxford University Press

Kennedy, I. and Grubb, A. (eds) (1998) *Principles of Medical Law*. Oxford University Press

Lewis, C. (1998) *Medical Negligence: A Practical Guide*, 4th Edn. Butterworths

Lugon, M. and Seeker, J. (1999) *Clinical Governance: Making it Happen*. Royal Society of Medicine Press

Roberts, G. and Holly, J. (1996) *Risk Management in Healthcare*. Witherby and Co. Ltd

Smith, J. (1999) *Smith and Hogan Criminal Law*, 9th Edn. Butterworths

Vincent, C. (ed.) (1995) *Clinical Risk Management*. BMJ Publishing Group

Index